CHOCOLATES
FOR THE PILLOWS

NIGHTMARES
FOR THE GUESTS

CHOCOLATES
FOR THE PILLOWS

NIGHTMARES
FOR THE GUESTS

The Failure of the Hotel Industry
to Protect the Traveling Public
from Violent Crime

KENNETH LANE PRESTIA

Bartleby Press
Silver Spring, Maryland

Printed in the United States of America

Published and Distributed by:

Bartleby Press
11141 Georgia Avenue
Silver Spring, Maryland 20902

Library of Congress Cataloging-in-Publication Data

Prestia, Kenneth Lane, 1938–
     Chocolates for the pillows, nightmares for the guests:
the failure of the hotel industry to protect the traveling
public from violent crime / Kenneth Lane Prestia.
          p.   cm.
     ISBN 0-910155-25-9 (pbk.)   : $12.95
     1. Hotels—Security measures.   I. Title.
TX911.3.S4P74   1993
363.2'89—dc20   93-5928
                                                        CIP

To the cherished memory of
FRANK A. PHELPS, CMP

It is because we put up with bad things that hotelkeepers continue to give them to us.

—Anthony Trollope

Contents

Foreword

I t was not unusual when my colleague Kenneth Prestia telephoned me because we share similar management backgrounds in lodging security and we have kept in touch over the years. It was the substance of his call that was unusual; he disclosed that he was writing a manuscript concerning security in the lodging industry. It became clear from our conversation that it would differ significantly from previous books concerning the subject. It would address the lodging industry's response to the problem of the protection of guests, employees and patrons. He would be writing about conditions that have existed throughout the industry for many years. More important, however, he would be writing about how these conditions continue to adversely affect those who use the services and accommodations of the industry.

When a draft copy of the manuscript was forwarded to me for review, I was not surprised by what I read, because I know from my own experience that the conditions described in this book exist in countless hotels and motels. I was, however, surprised and honored when I was asked to prepare this foreword.

I have reviewed the content of this book very carefully, and I am personally familiar with a number of the cases that are described. While it is not my nature to agree with anything 100 percent, I found this book to be factual and accurate.

It tells the story of the lodging industry's duty to provide a standard of reasonable care in the protection of its guests, employees and patrons. It identifies security measures that need to be implemented to meet that standard of care. It explains why anything less is unacceptable. It discloses that the industry as a whole is far behind acceptable standards.

If reading this book causes concern, as it should, then you

will realize the importance of becoming involved in your own security, as well as that of family members who may be traveling with you. Until the lodging industry accepts full responsibility for providing reasonable care—you must be especially aware. Awareness of your surroundings at all times, whenever you are a guest of any lodging establishment, is a necessary measure to help ensure that you do not become a victim of crime. On the other hand, your lack of vigilance, together with the unwillingness of a particular hotel or motel to provide reasonable care to protect you from harm, may very well result in tragedies like those you will read about in *Chocolates for the Pillows—Nightmares for the Guests*.

People have the power to change unacceptable conditions. As a consumer, you can influence positive change by either spending or withholding your dollars based upon whether or not you are offered safe accommodations and by choosing only travel agents who offer the safest accommodations in locations that are known to be low-risk. The insurance industry can make a positive contribution by insuring only the safest hotels and motels. These are examples of people working together to change unacceptable conditions.

The lodging industry itself is capable of contributing more than anyone. For many years it has needed to develop a written code of security standards for the protection of the public. The major corporations should have these standards signed by the CEO and displayed in all properties for guests to see. General managers and operating directors of hotels and motels should have their compensation reduced if they fail to implement these standards. Their continued failure to do so should result in their termination for non-performance and dereliction of duty. Industry corporations that franchise their corporate names to independent operators should mandate these standards within all franchise agreements. At present, franchise agreements, in one way or another, mandate a variety of standards. They range from the number of bars of soap and clothes hangers provided for the guest, to the design of outdoor signs. It is not an unreasonable expectation that franchise agreements mandate security standards for the public's safety.

These conditions do not exist in the lodging industry today, but they could tomorrow—if the industry leadership wanted them to exist. If they did, we could all enjoy the chocolates on the pillows much more than we do now, because we would all enjoy safer vacations and business travel accommodations that the industry is capable of providing.

Thank you, Kenneth, for your honesty and sincerity in authoring this book. Your effort to help make future lodging conditions safer, therefore better, is understandable. It is, however, going to require the efforts of many other concerned people to bring about needed changes to the industry's policies and practices.

Belleair, Florida
March 1993

Thomas E. Kindler

Thomas E. Kindler is formerly Corporate Director of Security for The Sheraton Corporation. During his tenure with Sheraton Hotels, he served the innkeeping industry as Chairman of the Security and Safety Committee of the American Hotel & Motel Association. Originally from Indiana, where he graduated from the University of Notre Dame, Mr. Kindler is currently President of Thomas Kindler Associates in Belleair, Florida, where he resides with his family.

Introduction

No industry that serves the American public is richer in history, grander in scope, or more important in function, than the innkeeping industry. It provides a basic human necessity; shelter. All across the U.S.A. in cities and towns large and small—along the myriad miles of connecting roads and highways—hotels and motels continue to serve as a welcome respite for the weary traveler.

Hotels across the nation that have been designated as historic landmarks remain in operation today. The Red Lion Inn in Stockbridge, Massachusetts, served as a stagecoach stop in 1773. The Menger, in San Antonio, was built adjacent to the Alamo in 1859 and has counted among its guests Sam Houston as well as Presidents Taft and McKinley. The St. Francis opened in 1904. One of the few structures to survive the San Francisco earthquake of 1906, it was reopened nineteen months later. The La Concha in Key West, Florida, opened in 1926. Tennessee Williams completed *A Streetcar Named Desire* while a guest. Charles Lindberg and Amelia Earhart were frequent visitors to the Hay Adams in Washington, D.C., built in 1927. These innkeeping properties, along with many others, have preserved their fascinating past, as well as their economic vitality.

In today's world of modern innkeeping, it is difficult to imagine earlier days when hotels lacked private baths and telephones first appeared only in public hallways and lobbies. In 1906, Ellsworth Milton Statler introduced private baths in his hotels by advertising "Room with a bath for a dollar and a half."

Numerous members of the industry conduct the business of innkeeping consistent with the responsibilities associated with their public trust. By their conduct, they honor the legendary hotelkeepers of bygone years, who became American success stories through their vision, hard work and ethics.

This book, however, is not about industry icons who became legends; nor is it concerned with those who sustain their ethical precepts. This book is about the conduct of ordinary hotelkeepers. It is about their failure to provide reasonable care to protect the public from harm at the hand of violent criminals.

Nearly twenty years ago, a national hotel corporation opened a prestigious new property in the Nation's Capital. It has hosted heads of state, noted celebrities, and several U.S. presidents. Interestingly enough, however, public records reveal that this hotel has not been immune from the results of spiraling city-wide crime statistics. In fact, a number of guests, as well as employees, have been victimized even by brutal and violent crime. When this hotel opened, it employed a significant number of security officers. Today, however, that number is less, while room rates are more. There are fewer security officers at a time when criminals have grown more arrogant and violent crime has grown more rampant. Yet, this hotel recently underwent a multi-million dollar renovation. There obviously is something inherently wrong about the triumph of aesthetics over the substance of security for the guest. This kind of obscure negligence is not unique to this particular hotel. On the contrary, it is illustrative of industrywide conditions. Anyone who seriously doubts this need only research the security conditions of hotels and motels within their own communities. Unfortunately, the same lack of knowledge that precipitates the need for answers seriously limits the ability of the public, as well as professionals who plan meetings and conventions, to ask appropriate questions of hotelkeepers regarding their security. Hopefully, this book will help remedy this situation. While a few national chains have embarked upon glacial-paced programs of improvement, it should be realized that the aim of public safety can not be achieved by a few hotel chains acting in isolation from the industry as a whole.

Those who use the accommodations and services of the industry, do so under a false sense of security. This is because crime is one of the best kept secrets of hotelkeepers. The industry's security problems are the result of its members ignoring the growing number one social issue of the past several decades—violent crime. The best paid minds in the industry have remained unquestioned about their motives and competency regarding the problem of guest security. Hotelkeepers continue to enjoy a tacit immunity from scrutiny or accountability, with respect to guest security policies and practices that directly affect the public's safety. And over the years, industry apologists have promoted a public relations charade of voluntary reform that has resulted in an ever deepening dilemma for all concerned. The industry's response to the problems of guest security is unacceptable. Year after year, serious guest security-related lawsuits continue to surface with consistency in courtrooms across the nation. And as any astute investigator knows, consistency does not indicate coincidence; it suggests predictability. As the industry lurches uncontrolled into the future, there is no determined purpose, sure swift tack, or collective resolve to end its problems over guest security.

Industry advertising does not sell a product; it sells a service. Inherent in this advertising is a promise—an assurance—of a secure environment. Innkeeping is a service industry, and service begins with fundamentals. Nothing is more fundamental to guest service than security.

Perhaps in the far future, the public will travel within that groundless frontier of outer space where the weight of luggage will be less and cosmotel will become a neologism. In any event, hotelkeepers today, as well as in the future, have but one fixed and inviolable duty. To that vital duty, all other services great and small offered to the public, are but corollary in nature. That duty is to provide reasonable care to protect guests, employees and patrons from the foreseeable risk of injury or death.

Violent crimes inflicted upon guests are disclosed in detail, drawn mostly from the evidence revealed in the resulting lawsuits. The names of the victims have either been altered or omitted out of respect for their privacy, except in two instances. One is the Connie Francis case because of its widespread publicity and the willingness of Ms. Francis to help others by discussing her nightmare with the media. The other is the case of the robbery and murder of Daniel "Duke" Hope. His mother, Theodora Michaud, requested the name of her beloved son be used. That request was honored.

In some cases that are examined, settlement resulted in a court order prohibiting the public disclosure of the identity of the litigants. These non-disclosure or "gag orders" have been respected and the names of the hotels or motels involved have been omitted. However, where names of hotels or motels have been identified, there is no intention to single out or deride a particular property or chain. They are simply symbolic of prevalent, industrywide conditions. Also omitted is the name of any hotel or motel where an employee provided verifiable information and specifically requested the property's name not be used.

There is no pretense of impartiality in the presentation of the content of this book—it is written from an informed bias that has developed from years of experience with the subject matter. No particular case can be recalled that prompted the decision to write about the industry's dilemma. As in filling a fine crystal glass, drop by drop, there is at last a drop that causes it to run over—so it is that in a series of experiences, there is at last one that causes the sense of concern to run over.

In a corner of my thoughts, I sometimes contemplate the criminal mind; the capacity to inflict heinous acts upon others. No doubt, each is destined—in a dimension of being yet to be experienced—to make peace with the victim, and, with greater difficulty, peace with themselves.

In the evening of my memories, however, I listen in vain for an inner silence. For I hear again the faraway voices of the victims. In my mind's eye, I see their image. My sight, however, is not focused upon the darkness of the experience they endured—but on their innocence and trust. For me there will continue to be the victims. In many respects this book is their story. It also echoes the story of many of my colleagues with whom it has been my privilege to be associated.

Numerous former and current colleagues and associates have encouraged me to write this book. Many friends, some within the hospitality industry and the law enforcement community, have added their voices of encouragement. Many of them must remain anonymous. The views expressed in this book may not be in full accord with everyone who has encouraged my effort, however, I have endeavored to be worthy of their trust by writing with a fidelity to the truth as I understand it.

My sincere gratitude to Sandra K. Lehman, Tom Kindler, Al Fury, Ed Quinn, Willie Grimes, Elaine Curl Gillespie, Mary Sullivan Mann and Edward Kielty for their valuable assistance. My appreciation is expressed to my publisher whose skills are evident on every page. And special acknowledgement of Francis Allen Phelps, who trusted and encouraged me to write.

One

Shocking The Conscience

Described by his colleagues as a brilliant physician and scientist, Dr. John Woodward Emerson was a research physician associated with a renowned cancer research institution in New York. He was a remarkable human being. At the early age of just two and a half years, he was able to read. At the youthful age of thirty-three, he was devoting his life to alleviating suffering. Dr. Emerson was the only child of an elderly English couple, who resided just outside London.

On a chilly Friday evening in February, 1976, Dr. Emerson was on a well earned, if brief, vacation with his longtime friend, Robert Jay McCormack. The two men decided to stop overnight in Norfolk, Virginia. It was about six o'clock in the evening when the two travelers spotted the big, bright motel sign off Virginia Beach Boulevard and decided to stop and check in.

Robert went inside the motel front office, while John remained outside in his Mercedes, which bore tags indicating he was a medical doctor. As McCormack registered at the front desk reception area, the New York schoolteacher inquired about directions to a particular restaurant. Uncertain about the location, the motel receptionist assured Robert that he would be contacted. As the two vacationers drove the short distance to their ground floor guest room, neither of them had any reason to suspect that the motel they had chosen had been subject to numerous crimes over the years; nor did either man have reason to fear that one of them was destined for a deadly checkout.

Once inside their comfortable room, the two men unpacked their luggage, relaxed, and discussed their anticipated

1

evening ahead. It was John who first decided to shave and freshen up. The bathroom was located immediately to the right upon entering the room from outside. As John shaved, Robert lounged on his bed while he watched TV and awaited directions from the front desk.

Just a few feet outside John and Robert's room, another motel guest, James Owens, was parking his car. His guest room was adjacent to the one occupied by the doctor and his friend.

As Mr. Owens parked his car, he could not help noticing two young men standing near his room. As he turned off the ignition key, he carefully observed the youth's dress and manner and concluded there was a danger present. With fear and apprehension, Mr. Owens sat in his car for several more moments milling around in his mind what to do. The actions of the youths influenced his decision. Aware of being observed, they walked away from Owens and his room. At that point, Mr. Owens decided to take a calculated risk. With room key ready, he made a dash to his room. Once inside, he locked the door and used the guest room telephone to do what virtually every industry security expert who ever defended a hotelier in litigation has claimed the guest should do under such circumstances— he reported the suspicious youths to a motel employee. He described them and conveyed his fear and concern.

As McCormack relaxed and Emerson shaved in the bathroom, there was a loud knock on their guest room door. In anticipation of receiving directions from the motel receptionist, Robert quickly left the bed to open the door. He was surprised to find two youths standing in front of him. One youth asked for someone by name. Explaining that no one by the name given was known to him, Robert started to close the door. He was startled as one youth attempted to force his way inside. Robert, who was a large man, and weighed nearly two hundred and forty pounds, clearly had the advantage of size and succeeded in pushing the door to within a few inches of closing. But, success was short-lived. The small space between the edge of the door and the door frame permitted enough room for the assailant's gun hand and when he pulled the trigger, a bullet ripped into Robert, the impact of the projectile forced him backward to the floor. As the two gunmen rushed inside, John Emerson emerged from the bathroom. Without hesitating, the gunman shot the doctor in the head. The impact of this shot dropped John where he stood. The gunmen stepped over him and wasting no time, ransacked the room, removed cash from their victims, and quickly departed. In dire pain and in a state of shock, the doctor's large traveling companion dragged himself to the telephone, dialed the front desk operator, and pleaded for help. Then he returned to his dying friend.

Suddenly, the two gunmen burst back into the room. Robert later described their frenzied efforts to remove their fingerprints from the room, using Robert's clothing to do so. Again, the gunmen hastily departed the crime scene. But, unlike their first exit, this second departure was observed by the unarmed motel security officer responding to the crime.

The elderly security officer, alone on patrol duty, gave chase across the motel parking lot, but he was no match for the youthful, fleet-footed gunmen. Considering the fact that he was unarmed, his lack of enthusiasm for the chase is quite understandable. The motel management regarded two-way radio communication for the security officer as an unnecessary expense, so that the officer was at a distinct disadvantage with the simple pager he had been furnished. He promptly proceeded to the guest room's macabre scene. Fortunately, the robbers had not disabled the telephone as is routinely done by criminals—the security officer used it to summon the police and an ambulance and help soon arrived.

Both John and Robert were taken to a nearby hospital emergency room. Robert required major emergency surgery to save his life. He would later require extensive medical treatment for his near fatal gunshot wound. John, who had been able to read at the tender age of two and a half years, was dead from a massive head wound, at age thirty-three; murdered in a strange city, inside a strange motel room.

Immediately following this brutal robbery and murder, the police conducted an investigation, resulting in the arrest of two suspects. Both were indicted by a Norfolk grand jury. The eighteen year old suspect was acquitted during a criminal trial. As a result of this acquittal, criminal charges against his twenty-two year old accomplice were dropped by the prosecuting attorney's office. Presumably, the killers of Dr. Emerson remain at large today.

Mr. and Mrs. Edward Emerson, the parents of the decedent, were devastated by the murder of their only child. The sanctimonious assertion by industry apologists that the number of violent criminal attacks upon guests are minimal compared to the total number of guests the industry serves, pales considerably when the grief and suffering of the victims or their survivors is considered. This assertion is of little solace, when one considers that violent crime would occur less often if hotelkeepers consistently exercised the degree of care the industry should provide.

During an emotional healing process, the decedent's parents sought the sum of $2,500 from the motel, in order to defray expenses for their son's funeral. In an informal settlement agreement, the motel consented to pay, but the sum agreed upon in good faith by the doctor's parents was never paid because the motel management heeded unwise advice from their attorneys. These attorneys informed the motel that the agreement was technically improper. To be valid in the Commonwealth of Virginia, such an agreement needed court approval. This had not been done, so the attorneys advised the motel not to pay the amount. The motel followed their attorney's advice, assuming that Mr. and Mrs. Emerson would find difficulty in taking action from the other side of the Atlantic Ocean. A Norfolk Circuit Court judge subsequently rendered a decision in favor of the motel.

But this was not the end of the bizarre scenario. The English couple may have been thwarted in the initial stage of their odyssey through the American judicial system, but they remained determined. The English are known for their tenacious spirit and in this instance, it saw the couple through to a good ending. In their quest for justice, the Emersons brought the matter before the Virginia Supreme Court, where their plight found sympathetic ears. The highest court of justice in Virginia overturned the lower court's decision and ordered the case to trial, whereupon the Emersons filed a two-million-dollar lawsuit against the motel, alleging that the motel had breached its duty to provide reasonable care, under the circumstances, to protect Dr. Emerson from foreseeable harm—death.

The trial took place six years after the motel murder of Dr. Emerson. It was conducted before a Norfolk Circuit Court jury of seven citizens. During the course of the four-day trial, evidence was presented to the jury regarding various aspects of the security policies and practices of the motel. The evidence revealed that the defendant motel had experienced a number of crimes prior to the doctor's murder. The most damaging evidence during the trial pertained to conduct by motel employees. They never responded to the initial call for help from Mr. Owens, which placed the motel on notice of danger to all guests. The security officer responded to the call from McCormack after he and Dr. Emerson had been shot and robbed. This fact weighed heavily on the mind of each juror.

The chief counsel for the motel's legal team claimed that Dr. Emerson was not a registered guest of the motel. He argued that the motel room had been rented to Mr. McCormack as a single room. Mr. McCormack's registration card was submitted into evidence, indicating the motel guest room had been rented from the motel as a single occupancy. However, this issue was disputed by McCormack. He stated that during registration he had told the clerk that the room was to be occupied by two individuals. Plaintiff's counsel argued that the motel, as an innkeeping establishment, was responsible for the reasonable security of even an invitee merely visiting a guest's room. This point is an established legal concept.

After three hours of deliberation, the jury of three men and four women awarded $500,000 to the mother and the same amount to the father of Dr. John Woodward Emerson. At the time of this one-million-dollar award, it was recognized by veteran court observers to be the largest guest security court award in the history of Virginia.

During post-verdict motions before the Norfolk Circuit Court, a defense attorney in a display of arrogance, was quoted as saying, "The amount shocks the conscience of a fair-minded person." The case underwent the appeals process in 1982. One claim in the defendant's appeal was that the award amount was excessive. The parents of Dr. Emerson were not growing younger and by the time a person reaches his seventies, time is a precious commodity. Eventually, they decided to settle the case against the motel for a lesser amount.

In many aspects, this Norfolk case is a microcosm of the innkeeping industry's dilemma over guest security. From the evidence presented, it is obvious that the jurors understood what had eluded the motel's management; the plain truth that innkeeping guest security is not always required to succeed—it is required to be reasonable.

An Elusive Issue

During the past two decades, a renewed public interest in matters bearing directly upon the issue of hotel-motel guest security and the public's safety has developed. Emerging is an expanded view of industry guest security policies and practices shocking to the conscience of a fair-minded person.

Factors common to the innkeeping industry directly affect the foreseeability of violent criminal attack upon the hotel-motel guest. Specifically, these factors are: (1) Innkeeping industry advertising; it sells a service, not a product. Inherent in this service, is the assurance of protection. (2) The transient nature of the guest impedes effective police investigation of crime and the successful prosecution of suspects. (3) The fact that guests of hotels and motels usually carry on or about their person, unusual amounts of cash, credit cards, jewelry and other valuables. This makes guests desirable targets for crimes of profit that are often violent in nature. (4) The absence of crime deterrence measures in the structural and landscaping design of hotels and motels has created environments that attract criminals. The commingling of these four factors gives rise to conditions that permit violent criminal attack.

It is well recognized by those trying to reduce violent crime, that society at large must support any government efforts. This includes the business community, in which the giant innkeeping industry is a major force. A recent judicial decision that mentioned innkeeper-guest relationships and addressed the growing concern for escalating violent crime, stated in part: "We note that in the fight against crime, the police are not expected to do it all; every segment of society has an obligation to aid law enforcement, and to minimize the opportunities for crime." But the response by the vast majority of hotelkeepers to violent crime against their guests has been scattered, with individual interpretation of scope, cause, effect and solution. This response by the industry is unacceptable. The industry is finding it increasingly difficult to silence this fact.

In September of 1977, the Domestic and International Administration of the U.S. Department of Commerce issued a small report entitled "Crime in Service Industries." As far as it is known, this is the only U.S. government publication of its kind. Chapter Five of this report covers crime in the innkeeping industry, and in part, examines violent crimes against guests. According to this report, the crimes of assault, robbery, rape and murder result in industry losses attributable to claim payments, lawsuits, increased insurance payments, decreased occupancy rates, as well as significant loss of reputation. The report states that at the time it was written, there were roughly 45,000 commercial hotel and motel establishments throughout the United States and that national chains accounted for over forty percent of the total number of rooms offered to the public. These figures have increased significantly since this report was issued. In fact, at present there is an overcapacity in the innkeeping industry. Too many rooms and too few guests have forced the industry to consolidate.

To a certain degree, the government report appears biased, perhaps because the industry itself was consulted to a great extent for the information in it. Taking advantage of this publication, the industry has included excerpts from the report in various publications available to industry members because information in the report addresses the important issues of the protection of assets and inventory loss prevention. Conspicuously absent in the industry publications is the summary of this 1977 government report. The short poignant summary reads as follows:

> The impact of crime on the lodging industry is severe enough for it to be an irrefutable cause of establishment failure, according to one industry source. Given the nature of the service produced, and the extraordinary vulnerability to crime, this industry should act more progressively in preventing the opportunities that create crime. The uniqueness of the service does not exempt its crime from the preventable category.
>
> To control what surely will be escalating crime, the industry initially must develop a loss measurement and analysis approach. It also must overcome the fear that customer alienation will result from application of progressive security policies. In succumbing to this rationale, industry managers overlook both the public concern over crime and the industry capacity to ameliorate the impact of crime control through public education.

The performance record of the industry during the past two decades regarding the issue of guest security provides ample reason for concern. While there has been some improvement, industry policies and practices leave much to be desired. There is an abundance of evidence to suggest that guests have been the victims of violent crime in ever increasing numbers. This evidence, however, is obscured by several considerations that bear directly on any attempt to assess either the extent, or the seriousness of the problem. Among these considerations, the most significant are the following: (1) All violent crime committed against hotel-motel guests is not reported to law enforcement authorities. The chief barriers to faithful reporting of crime are police and criminal court procedures as well as potential publicity. This is particularly true of the crimes of forcible rape or attempted rape, where the victim's perception of public stigma reduces the frequency with which these crimes are reported. Additionally, guests of hotels and motels are often reluctant to commit the time and money necessary to return to the jurisdiction where they were victimized, and to assist the police in their investigation or prosecution of suspects. (2) When notified, some hotelkeepers will attempt to assuage the consequences of a criminal attack on a guest through the use of administrative remedy. Such remedy invariably will include the victim immediately being provided complimentary room accommodations and reimbursement for monetary loss. (3) Victims who do report crime to authorities usually do not file lawsuits. Civil court procedures and potential publicity, as well as financial considerations, reduce the number of lawsuits. Legal costs often outweigh demonstrable injury. Some lawsuits cannot be justified from a financial perspective, because the expenses associated with the litigation process exceeds the value of the claim. (4) The vast majority of lawsuits that are filed are effectively removed from public scrutiny, because they are settled out-of-court. (5) Increasing numbers of hotelkeepers, especially those self-insured, are settling personal injury claims before a lawsuit is even filed. This is being done because of the industry experience of few courtroom victories; higher insurance deductibles that require hotelkeepers, who are not self-insured, to pay a higher initial share of claims; and the increasing costs associated with defending against allegations in a lawsuit. (6) There is no nationwide public or private organization that indexes statistics for the crimes of robbery by force, aggravated assault, forcible rape, or murder committed against guests in hotels or motels.

Notwithstanding the foregoing considerations, guest security-related lawsuits filed against members of the industry have become the nemesis of negligent hotelkeepers. Such lawsuits provide a window into the industry's guest security practices . The testimony of industry managers, as well as their subordinates, and their admissions of negligence, are devastating to the public relations aspects of the business.

Neither the issue of violent criminal attack upon guests, nor the extensive level of its occurrence, are matters of mere blind speculation; each is a matter of meticulous investigation and common sense. Just as each granule of sand doesn't need to be examined to recognize a beach, likewise, every innkeeping property doesn't need to be examined to recognize dangerous industry conditions. Consistently, year after year, issues of guest security surface in federal and state courts across the nation. As any astute investigator knows, consistency does not indicate coincidence; it suggests predictability.

Virtually every step taken to investigate and verify provides a coherent and comprehensive picture of unsafe conditions far greater in scope than ordinarily believed to exist. They are conditions the industry is silent about and tries to keep hidden. The industry maintains a code of silence on crime. Breaking this code of silence and discovering evidence of the industry's dilemma over guest security is not a simple task.

With the exception of the National Fire Incident Reporting System, which indexes the crime of arson, no national organization public or private indexes crime statistics concerning guests of hotels and motels. But, various law enforcement agencies with sophisticated computerized crime reporting systems can identify, by addresses, where crimes are reported. In this way, crime statistics of specific innkeeping properties in a given jurisdiction may be tabulated by means of a computerized printout, which furnish the address, date, and type of crime reported. Ordinarily, the general public cannot obtain such data upon request. Attorneys involved in hotel or motel lawsuits can obtain such information by court order. Upon request and as a courtesy, it is often furnished to industry associations of security practitioners.

In 1981, at a West Coast meeting of industry security practitioners, a crime report was disseminated among the attendees of a top-level committee meeting. This report showed that in San Francisco, during 1980, the city's twenty major hotels reported 1,517 crimes. This figure was broken down into several categories: Homicides 1; rapes 2; robberies 12; and assaults 52. The bulk of the remaining crimes were burglaries. While the report did not specify how many of the crimes were committed specifically against the hotels' guests, it is reasonable to assume that guests were the victims of virtually all the crimes reflected in the report. It should be kept in mind that these figures reflect the twenty major hotels and do not reveal the total number of crimes reported by all hotels and motels within the city limits of San Francisco.

Two randomly selected major hotels in the Northwest section of Washington, D.C., offer additional insights. They reported a total of 145 crimes to the District of Columbia Metropolitan Police during 1989. Among these crimes, the police classified 15 as robberies, 5 as assaults, and 1 as arson.

In many jurisdictions, law enforcement officers who take a written report from a complainant often may exercise discretion in classifying a reported crime. On any given date, several guest rooms in a given hotel may be unlawfully entered and items stolen while the guests sleep. In some instances, police reports for the several crimes on that date will show only one burglary for the hotel address, but will list the several crimes as larcenies. Thus, serious felonies, such as burglary, where a dwelling is actually occupied, can be reduced—but only on paper. It is estimated that, on average, each hotel and motel room in the U.S. is illegally entered 4 times every year.

A survey of veteran business travelers, conducted by *Corporate Travel* magazine, and published in its November 1992 issue may help clarify the extent of crime incidence. Among the results: Nearly 24% of the respondents said they had been a victim of hotel crime, almost half of them within the past two years; nearly 40% of non-victims reported that a companion or associate had been victimized; almost 9% stated they knew someone who had been assaulted in a hotel; and 3% stated that an associate had been either sexually assaulted or raped in a hotel.

In a 1991 article, Kevin Helliker, staff reporter for the *Wall Street Journal*, wrote in part: " With no outcry over the issue, the Federal Bureau of Investigation and other law enforcement agencies, which for years have tracked convenience-store crime, don't keep statistics on hostelry crime. And the industry itself won't reveal any statistics. 'Each company considers its crime statistics proprietary,' says Ray Ellis, director of risk management and operations for the American Hotel & Motel Association, a trade group."

Reasonable Care

The current guest security problem did not develop overnight. It is the direct result of the vast majority of hotelkeepers having ignored the growing number one social issue of the past several decades—violent crime.

Traditionally, the terms hotel, motel, inn, lodge, motor lodge, and motor inn are used synonymously to describe structures providing sleeping accommodations for the public on an interim basis. In many jurisdictions they are defined by statute. Wherever a statutory description exists, it supersedes subjective and historical interpretation.

As long ago as ancient Egypt, establishments providing public accommodation and furnishing the necessities of food, shelter, and protection have reported violent criminal attack upon guests. During the Middle Ages, the English inn appeared, and in time a body of English common law to address the relationship between innkeeper and guest. This traditional English common law serves as the foundation for American legal concepts about innkeeping. Embodied within American innkeeping law is the clear duty of the innkeeper to provide the guest with reasonable care against foreseeable risk of harm.

Reasonable care has been defined as the commission or omission of acts or conditions, which are prudent and reasonable, under the circumstances, to protect the guest from foreseeable harm, or loss of property. The innkeeper, however, is not construed as the insurer of the guest's personal safety; nor is the innkeeper responsible for protecting the guest from all possible harm. But, the innkeeper, as well as his employees, has a moral and legal duty to protect the guest against the risk of harm that is revealed through the exercise of reasonable care.

The services provided the guest by the innkeeper are conducted on an interim basis and are transitory in character. This distinguishes the innkeeper-guest relationship from that of landlord-tenant.

The judiciary has demonstrated a trend toward holding hoteliers responsible for increasingly stricter standards of care. In a decision on May 1, 1979, the Wisconsin Supreme Court, remanded a case back to trial court, in rendering an opinion typical of this judicial trend. The case involved a guest robbed at a Holiday Inn in Wauwatosa, Wisconsin. The court stated: "Certainly hotel patrons can expect that reasonable security will be provided, combined with the friendliness, hospitality, and graciousness so widely advertised by modern hotels." Reasonable care and reasonable security are synonymous. The court went on to offer that hotel or motel circumstances might require such security measures as the employment of security personnel, closed circuit television surveillance, dead-bolt locks on guest room doors, as well as security doors on entrances located some distance from the lobby entrance. The Wisconsin Supreme Court further stated in its opinion that one of the relevant considerations in deciding whether or not proper care has been provided, is the design of the buildings and landscape of a hotel or motel.

In a more recent court decision, the Fifth Circuit Court of Appeals, in 1984, upheld a lower court decision, holding a defendant hotel in New Orleans, Louisiana, liable for damages exceeding $900,000. At that time the hotel was operated by the Hyatt chain. The case involved the robbery and murder of a respected doctor. The case was a landmark decision because of the whereabouts of the guest when murdered—on a public sidewalk, about four feet from the hotel entrance. This case was deemed sufficiently important to the industry for the leading industry trade association, AH&MA, to enter an *amicus curiae*, (friend of the court) brief on behalf of the defendant hotel. But, the Appeals Court extended the legal duty of the hotel to provide security beyond the hotel premises, to the immediate area of the hotel's entrance. These and other such judicial opinions provide a wealth of insight into the industry's guest security negligence.

In recognition of contemporary social issues, both federal and state judiciaries have sought to influence hotelkeepers to eliminate dangerous policies and practices. By their activism, judges have been and remain a marked contrast to legislators at all levels—municipal, state and federal—who typically ignore public safety issues of the lodging industry.

With increasing awareness, the judiciary acknowledges that innkeepers, as well as their managers, control their premises, and therefore, have the power to act; the power to effect positive change. For example, innkeepers, their managers and employees, have responsibility to select, purchase, install and maintain the locks on guest room doors and are custodians of the keys that open the locks. Further, the innkeepers and their managers recruit, hire, train, and retain employees. Guests are not in control of such matters; nor are they in control of a wide spectrum of other security matters of paramount importance to their safety.

Additionally, innkeepers and their subordinates either know, or should know, the nature and frequency of violent crime on and about the hotel-motel premises. Ordinarily, the guest, often traveling from great distances and sometimes residing in small communities experiencing minimal crime, would not possess the knowledge necessary to modify his or her behavior. The truth is that almost all hotels and motels withhold information concerning crime, especially violent crime on or about the premises, in the fear that releasing such information would result in a serious decline in occupancy. Members of the industry withhold this information despite the fact that danger to the guest grows no greater once he or she is informed.

Generally, the innkeeper is construed to be the proprietor, who conducts the business of innkeeping. As such, the innkeeper cannot abrogate his legal duty to provide reasonable care for the guest by simply delegating this duty to subordinates because the innkeeper and his managers, are deemed vicariously liable for negligent acts associated with the official discharge of their employees' duties. Indeed, among their varied duties, employees are provided for the very purpose of protecting the guest from foreseeable harm.

Where public safety statutes, ordinances, or codes exist, they do not necessarily ensure reasonable care. They represent minimum standards of compliance and are frequently enacted as the result of political influence. On the other hand, where statutes, ordinances or codes are enacted and enforced consistent with judicial decisions, an intrinsically greater opportunity exists that hotelkeepers will avoid penalties when complying with these rules.

Only a handful of the regional and national hotel-motel chains own the hotels or motels bearing their well-advertised name and familiar logos. Throughout the late sixties and seventies, many hotel-motel companies divested themselves of ownership, so that currently the majority of the well-known chains operate as either a management company or a franchisor. Through management contracts, rather than actual ownership, the major chains can expand faster with considerably less investment of capital per property. In addition, it should be noted that some of the smaller hotel and motel management companies exist as subsidiaries of larger ones. Many of the hotels and motels managed by the large, elite chains are actually owned by companies formed by several entrepreneurs; while others are owned by institutional entrepreneurs, for example, some of the giant corporations of the insurance industry. Franchising has become increasingly popular because the major hotel and motel chain franchisors offer the business person unique opportunities for success. The most obvious benefits are instant name and trademark recognition by the traveling public through nationwide advertising, as well as access to a vast reservations network, a vital marketing tool.

The industry of innkeeping concerns itself less with public hospitality than with earning profit. But it must be recognized, even acknowledged, that some hotelkeepers understand that harm can result from policies and practices that place profit before public safety.

Conscientious and earnest members of the industry comprise a minority. As a result, the industry's tenet of voluntary guest security reform is an atrocious failure. This voluntary reform gave birth to the industry's problems over guest security that have, for years, been nurtured and perpetuated by the industry's "excuse" managers. These "excuse" managers draw attention away from the failures of voluntary guest security reform in order to serve corporate profit interests.

The "excuse" managers are vociferously supported by a sizeable cadre of industry apologists. The most visible industry apologists, industry trade association bureaucrats, act as minions for the industry's corporate leaders. Joining them are various members of the academic community. Neither group has direct, "hands on" experience with guest security; but both groups are eager to influence others by explaining what they have learned secondhand. Often, members of the academic community, affiliated with colleges of hotel administration, are supported by the industry in a variety of ways. It should not be inferred that all members of the academic community teaching hotel management are automatically industry apologists. They are not. In personal correspondence with the author, a professor of Hotel Management at Cornell University wrote in part: "Most of us really do not understand the responsibilities of the security department—how delicate, and how broad they are—at the same time—and your talks to the Hotel Operations classes enable a good percentage of our graduates to understand and relate to those responsibilities a little better."

The ordinary innkeeper knows little about hotel-motel guest security; and at the same time, the ordinary industry manager is ignorant of methodology used in guest security. What limited knowledge on the subject they do possess is only hearsay. Acquired secondhand, their knowledge is predisposed to error. Unfortunately, most managers believe that what they understand about guest security is all there is to be understood. The greater their ignorance of guest security, the greater is their suspicion of its effectiveness. Thus, they perpetuate the fallacious idea that the industry can do little to protect the guest from violent criminal attack. Many in positions of leadership and influence within the highest levels of industry operations are the very industry personnel responsible for the purchase and installation of thousands of unsafe locks for guest room doors in hotels and motels across the nation. It is foolish to suppose that industry managers are also security literate.

Security is perceived strictly as a non-revenue producing administrative function. As a result, there is a failure to consider security in the proper light; to see that security is a valuable management tool. Security can serve dual purposes—

reduce the incidence of violent criminal attack upon the guest, and simultaneously reduce the number of lawsuits resulting from such crimes.

If management uses security protocol at all, it is usually devoted to protecting assets and reducing inventory loss. Managers typically perceive these losses as bottom-line profit and loss figures. Indeed, employee defalcation and theft are serious management concerns. But they can never supersede the foremost concern; protection of guests and employees. The myopia on the part of management results in relegating guest security to a low priority in relation to other expenditures. They are unwilling to allocate the necessary labor costs associated with a viable, prudent, and reasonable guest security protocol. They fail to understand that their guests are entitled to protection. As a result, expenditures for landscaping, or a heated swimming pool, become more important than expenditures for safe guest room locks. Aesthetics are more imperative than safety in the competitive world of innkeeping.

The Harbinger

Collectively, members of the industry have demonstrated neither empathy with the victims of violent crime, nor a responsibility for violating the public trust. Meticulous examination of facts relevant to litigation against hoteliers often reveals startling behavior. For instance, it is not unheard of that victimized hotel guests are moved to a nearby hospital for admission, and upon discharge, they go directly home, whereupon, they are subsequently sent a bill from the hotel, unpaid as a result of the unfortunate method of their untimely checkout.

Criminal attacks upon guests often result in permanent physical impairment, serious psychological scars, even death. The victims of these attacks are not individuals without identity. They are not faceless—they are friends and neighbors, business associates, wives, husbands, children, brothers and sisters. But as the industry's memory of these sordid events fades, the industry spotlight shifts toward increasing insurance coverage, increasing room rates, and increasing profits. For many years, the hoteliers' pat answer to rising crime has been to purchase additional indemnification from insurers and then claim that they do not need more security—because they have insurance coverage. It has been a strategy of denial—a kind of reckless crapshoot with the public's safety. While this strategy worked, there was little motivation for managers to change their attitudes. They operated with a measure of immunity from penalties. That is, they did so until the Fall of 1974. For, at that time, a harbinger made its dramatic appearance and portended a revolutionary future course of events for the innkeeping industry.

Connie Francis was a very popular female vocalist who had earned a loyal following of devoted fans and admirers from coast to coast. During the Fall of 1974, she was emerging from partial retirement. In fulfilling not only her destiny, but unwittingly, the destiny of the innkeeping industry, she was a registered guest at the Howard Johnson's in Westbury, Long Island, New York, during the early morning hours of November 8, 1974. Ms. Francis retired at about 3:00 a.m. At about 4:00 a.m. she was awakened by an assailant, who placed a sharp knife at her throat. During the next two and a half hours she pleaded and bargained for her life, while she was terrorized, assaulted, and threatened with death. At about 6:30 a.m., the assailant escaped and has never been identified, arrested or prosecuted for this heinous crime. Within a short time she retained the legal counsel of Richard Frank, a prominent New York attorney, who filed a multi-million-dollar lawsuit against the hotel. In the suit, he alleged that the hotel had breached its legal duty to provide reasonable care, hence reasonable security, to protect her from the foreseeable risk of injury.

What distinguishes this lawsuit from all others preceding it, is the barbarism of the crime, coupled with the fame and popularity of the victim. These facts catapulted the case into the national news. The case commanded widespread public attention, and quickly became a major media event now legendary throughout the industry. This unique civil trial was lengthy, at times bordering a carnival atmosphere with stand-

ing room only for courtroom spectators. In fact, at one point
in the trial, the sympathetic judge barred members of the press
from the courtroom. But, within a few days, this ruling was
overturned through the efforts of attorneys arguing on behalf
of a press club. It was revealed that the defendant hotel had
experienced a number of criminal acts against its guests prior
to the attack upon the victim. In fact, on the same night of the
attack, two other guests had been victimized by an intruder.
On duty during this hotel horror was a lone employee, assigned
to work at the guest reception area in the hotel lobby.

The sliding glass door of the victim's guest room, which
allowed exit to the outside grounds, could be opened from the
outside with little effort, although it had been locked from the
inside. The hotel knew this, and attempted to remedy this haz-
ardous security condition by ordering new locks to replace the
deficient ones. The often repeated story by industry apologists
is that the new locks ordered by the hotel had been delayed in
transit because of a strike affecting the cargo carrier. This prevented the defendant hotel from taking timely delivery of the
new locks and installing them as planned. However, this explanation pales, when all the facts in the matter are examined.

Nearly six months after the attack of November 8, 1974,
the plaintiff's attorney obtained a court order to conduct an
inspection of the defendant hotel's premises. About half of the
hotel's sliding glass doors could still be opened from the outside while locked from the inside, including, ironically, the
guest room formerly occupied by the attorney's client.

The victim had suffered fear, anxiety, and depression
immediately following her nightmare attack. Subsequent to the
attack, the victim continued to suffer traumatic phobia, neuro-
sis and depression, which resulted in social withdrawal, according to the medical testimony. Obviously, these conditions are
a most difficult experience for one who earns his or her living
as an entertainer. It would be many years before Connie Francis would be able to pick up the shattered pieces of her life.

On July 1, 1976, a Federal court jury awarded her
$2,500,000. During post-verdict motions before the court, the
defense legal team sought to have the jury award set aside as

excessive. However, on September 20, 1976, the court upheld the award. Coincidentally, on this same day, a troubled executive committee of the American Hotel & Motel Association (AH&MA), convened in Woodstock, Vermont, and was provided with a detailed report from their legal counsel concerning this fateful guest security lawsuit.

It began to dawn upon even the most intellectually impoverished members of the industry that there was a willingness of juries to award substantial sums of money to victims of violent hotel crime. Most people familiar with this lawsuit agree that the case had a profound impact. Some hotelkeepers responded by actually improving guest security. Others merely created the illusion of improved protection. Unfortunately, many did absolutely nothing. But certainly, countless guests during the years since 1976, have benefited from the experiences of this "Harbinger." Hopefully, after many years of healing, this courageous woman will understand that her role as plaintiff fulfilled one of her true missions in this life, and also fulfilled her destiny as well. Upon reflection, she may rhetorically ask—"Who's sorry now?"

As crime escalated to epidemic proportions during the years since, increasing numbers of victimized guests participated in the litigation process. This resulted in monetary consequences for hoteliers in general, and negligent hoteliers in particular. The practical implications of the increasing numbers of lawsuits against the industry began to be understood by the insurance industry. Rather than develop guest security performance standards for hotelkeepers, which would have benefitted the public, the insurers simply began to evaporate. Varying levels of insurance protection, which provides indemnification against lawsuits resulting from the negligent conduct of hoteliers, began to dry up. The cap on indemnification increasingly became $1 million. Many re-insurance markets— companies offering greater coverage by sharing the risk, and then sharing part of the sizeable premium paid by the insured hotelier—also dried up. Higher and higher deductibles have required hoteliers to pay greater initial amounts in claims and settlements. Court judgments have become routine, much to the dismay and chagrin of industry members nationwide. The reaction by many of the elite national industry chains was to self-insure, leaving the smaller hoteliers to fend for themselves in an increasingly costly insurance market. Recently the States of Illinois and New York have compelled innkeepers to increase liability insurance and the list of states doing so is increasing.

Industry members, and their insurers, have become increasingly adept at defending their interests in the courtroom. However, losses continue to outpace victories because the industry as a whole does little more than reclaim ground lost in the past. It should be kept in mind that courtroom drama such as that involving Mr. and Mrs. Emerson in Norfolk, represents a fraction of litigation simply because the vast majority of security-related lawsuits filed against hoteliers are settled long before they reach trial. Interesting enough, once a member of the industry is sued, the big question is not a matter of whether the hotelier wins or loses, but how the blame is concealed.

The stark truth is that few hotelkeepers concern themselves with guest security enough to institute nationwide reform. But very few hotelkeepers will publicly admit this fact. While the industry enjoys widespread influence throughout the business community and remains one of America's largest industries, it also holds the distinction of being one of the most unregulated American industries in regard to public safety.

Over a period of time, the public has come to expect more from the innkeeper. The public expects hotelkeepers to allocate sufficient funds for a hotel-motel environment that provides a minimal risk of violent criminal attack—with the cost for doing this equitably distributed among guests. This is neither a novel business concept, nor is it an abnormal expectation by the public. Innkeeping is a service industry, and service begins with fundamentals. Nothing is more fundamental to guest service than security.

Many hotelkeepers perceive the criminal attacking guests on their premises as the cause of security problems. It is not the cause. Other hotelkeepers regard hotel-motel crime victims, their attorneys and judicial activism, as causes of their dilemma. They are not causes either. None is the cause of guest security problems—all are the effects of it. The dilemma is not a condition imposed upon the industry membership by some force outside the industry. It is self-imposed. Like an immature child, the industry perceives itself as the victim of events caused by others. What is needed is for the industry to embark upon a journey of serious introspection. Such introspection is important at this time; for, as the industry continues a policy of business as usual by thwarting real guest security reform, another crisis looms just ahead. The specter of widespread government regulation is now becoming a reality. It hovers above the head of even the most conscientious and enlightened hotelier. The erosion of the industry stonewall of opposition to legislative action has already begun at the local level. Government officials, in greater numbers, are realizing that the public no longer can rely upon absent hotel entrepreneurs and short tenure mangers to be guardians of public safety. No one wants regulation, but it may become necessary because voluntary industry reform has failed. In 1982, the courageous board of supervisors of the City of San Francisco, passed Ordinance 6-82, which directly affects the security of all guests in hotels and motels within the San Francisco city limits. This Ordinance effectively amended the city's building code and mandated installation of dead-bolt locks on all guest room doors. San Francisco is not the only city to do this. It is the hotelkeeper's conduct that invites regulation.

While reasonable care and reasonable security are synonymous terms, neither needs to be defined by judicial fiat. Reasonable care is definitively written upon the conscience of each honest and moral hotelier. It speaks of caring. Hotelkeepers need to provide the reasonable care that they themselves would expect as hotel-motel guests.

The industry needs security performance standards. Voluminous judicial decisions have addressed the issue of reasonable care. It is this body of judicial wisdom that serves as a beacon of guiding light along the pathway of innkeeping law and the duty of the industry—*salus populi*—the safety of the people.

Two

The Concord Connection

Their lives were deeply rooted in an ancestry predating the Civil War era. Melissa and Thomas Butler had grown up, gone to school, married, and reared two sons in their tranquil, rural, community nestled in the beautiful Virginia countryside. Of course, their life together was not without challenges, yet the fact that they remained married for nearly half a century, bespeaks maturity and stability. But that stability would be shattered suddenly on a cold Friday evening, after they paid $58.04 for lodging in a motel in Concord, North Carolina.

The following are excerpts from the transcript of the sworn testimony of Melissa, concerning the nightmarish events on that February evening:

Q. Mrs. Butler, please state your full name for me.
A. Melissa Laura Lynn Butler.
Q. All right. What is your age right now, Mrs. Butler?
A. Seventy.
Q. And what was your age on February 27, 1981?
A. Sixty-six.
Q. Are you presently married?
A. Yes.
Q. To whom?
A. Thomas James Butler.
Q. How many times have you been married?
A. Just once.
Q. And when were you married?
A. May 29, 1936.
Q. Do you have any children?
A. Two.

Q. Both sons?

A. Two sons.

Q. And what are their ages?

A. One is 45 and one is 36.

Q. All right. What is your educational background: How far did you go in school?

A. I went through four years of college.

Q. Where did you go to college?

A. To Longwood College in Farmville.

Q. What did you do after college in the way of work?

A. Taught school in Windsor, Virginia, for one year.

Q. And after teaching, what happened?

A. I got married.

Q. When did you resume working, other than as a mother and housewife?

A. 1966. Full time.

Q. And now, where are you talking about you started going to work in 1966?

A. At our store in Virginia.

Q. Give us some history and background on it if you will, in terms of how long it has been there and how your husband acquired an interest in it.

A. Well the business, when we closed it, was 102 years old. It was started in 1881, and my husband's uncle came into the business soon after it started, as an employee, and in 1891 he became a part of—of the company. In 1944 my husband became president of the company. He worked at the store until he became Commissioner of Revenue in 1966.

Q. Can you tell the jury here in North Carolina what a Virginia commissioner of revenue is, and what he does?

A. Well they call him the "tax man". He's actually the person who keeps the land records straight, personal property.

Q. He's a state officer then?

A. Yes, he's a constitutional officer.

Q. All right. And when he left the position in 1966, what did you do?

A. I was at the store and more or less managed the store, well, really, operating the store.

Q. And at the time of this trip to North Carolina, in February of 1981, that you and your husband made, were you working at the store?

A. Yes.

Q. What was your position?

A. I was manager of the store.

Q. And was your husband retaining any title or office with the company?

A. Yes, he was president of the company.

Q. Even after he was commissioner of revenue?

A. Yes.

Q. And did you have a title or position as an officer in the company?

A. Yes I do. I was secretary and treasurer.

Q. In February 1981, you went to North Carolina. Where were you going, and what were your plans? What was the occasion for this trip?

A. To the Southern Living Show, in Charlotte. We had been there before, I liked it, and had an interest in gardening, and we decided to go back again.

Q. Some of the jurors may know what the Southern Living Show is, but I don't. Will you tell us what that is?

A. Well, it's actually a flower and—and a—the landscapes, homes, and it had a craft show connected with it.

Q. Did you make reservations in Charlotte, in advance of going?

A. We tried in Charlotte, but we got reservations in—for two nights—which were February 27 and 28—at the Holiday Inn in Concord.

Q. It was close enough to Charlotte and convenient to the activities that you were going to?

A. That's right.

Q. Did you spend Friday in Charlotte?

A. No, we went straight to the motel in Concord.

Q. Tell the members of the jury, if you can, about what time it was when you got to the Holiday Inn.

A. I'd say about 8:00 p.m.

Q. All right. And can you tell the members of the jury what

happened, that you can recall, from the time you pulled into the office at the Holiday Inn?

A. We stopped out front. We didn't go under the marquee, or awning, there was a parking place right there. My husband went in to register and came back out to get me to go in with him to pay for the two nights lodging because I had the—what do you call these checks you have?

Q. American Express?

A. Well not—

Q. Travelers checks?

A. Yes, travelers checks. So I went in and did that, and we both came back to the car and went around to the room. And we went round to the side to room 109.

Q. Was it dark at this time?

A. Yes, there were lights on under the shed of the motel.

Q. Where were you able to park your car?

A. Right at the door.

Q. And can you recall generally what it looked like in the way of the number of cars parked around there?

A. Well to my memory, I don't think there was a car on that row at all.

Q. What did you do once you parked the car?

A. We got things out—everything we had, we got out. And Tommy was out at the car fiddling around. But, anyway, by the time he got round to the trunk of the car, I looked to my left and saw a person turn the corner.

Q. Coming towards you?

A. To us, toward me. And my husband was locking the car and I said "Have you got everything out?" I didn't have any suspicion in my mind when I saw the man. Just give me a minute. And he came up to Tommy and said, "I want to ask you a question." And Tommy looked up, ready to answer the question, and with that, the man started pushing. And he pushed Tommy, pushed him over, pushed both of us in. He was a tall man. I was behind the door by that time, and he pushed me just against the wall, and pushed Tommy over by hitting at him. And the man turned the television up as loud as he could, I reckon, because you couldn't hear in there. He told Tommy to stay still, and told me to stay quiet, and he had a gun in his hand. Tommy was still on the floor, pleading with him to—you know—he could have what we had, just what he wants—and so forth. At that time, the man went to the door and said, "You all come on in." And two more men came in. And Tommy was knocked down by that lick the man gave him. He just socked Tommy.

Q. Did Tommy stay down?

A. No, he tried to get up and every time he did, they would knock him down again. He called for help so they hit him again. And then I was feeling dissolved by that time, you know, I mean, I didn't know whether I was going to faint— I was so afraid I was doing what they told me to do, which is what I—I would do. And then they—during this time they were, you know, just going through things. I saw things, but they did not want me to look up, and I was afraid to really. Before they pushed Tommy on the floor, they took his glasses off and stomped them, and broke them, and they did the same to mine a little bit later.

And then they pushed Tommy—the bed was here—and he pushed him right in the corner of the bed, down flat, and they tied him up with his arms and legs together behind him. And they put a gag thing around his mouth. And I think he gave up then; I really do, and then they covered him with blankets, and the mattress.

But—so they took me and they wanted to know if I had any money. And I told them yes, and I told them it was "in my pocketbook."

And then they said, "Well how about her?" I was still behind the door and the man grabbed me. And he said, "Well is he out?", or "How about him?" And the other man said, "Well, I have him fixed up. I mean, he is out." I felt that Tommy had just passed out over there, passed out as being knocked out. So they took me from behind the door, and put me on the other side, near a chair. And my glasses fell off when they threw me to the floor, and when I tried to reach for them, they stomped and broke those. I saw that I had lost them—and realized because I need my glasses. And they stomped them, stomped them and broke them.

And then the man put the gun to my neck. I was not resisting. And he told me to take off my watch and my ring, and he told me to give him whatever jewelry I had, and I gave him the watch, and then he said "the ring." and I could not get the ring off at first. It was an engagement ring, and I could not get it off at first.

Q. How long had you had that ring on?

A. Oh, how many years have I been married? I—over forty years.

Q. Why hadn't you been able to get it off in the past?

A. Well my fingers were big.

Q. Increased in size?

A. Yes—I yes—and I could not get it off, and he says "I will blow your brains out"—with the pistol right here at my neck—"if you don't take it off." And I pulled until I got it off. I had a scratch because the ring was broken underneath in a little place. And I told you they broke my glasses.

Q. Right.

A. Then the most frightening part to me was they—they did tie me up. They were using the sheets off the beds to tie me with. And they did take a handkerchief and kleenex from my pocketbook and put it in my mouth. And I pushed it out one time, and then they pushed it in again, and I could hardly breath. And then they said, "Let's go," and that was it. They left. And I do not know the lapse of time that was. I mean, I just don't know. I know it was alright; I got loose, my arms, and my legs, and the first thing I did was to put the latch on the door, that little thing that doesn't do much good, but it's there. And then I got the mattress off Tommy and I said, "I'm going to call for help before I untie you." It was dark in the room, and I didn't have my glasses. I dialed zero because I felt like that would get an operator.

Well, I could not get the operator and I didn't know how to get it, and couldn't see how to get it so I just "muggled" it. I mean I just kept on dialing all sorts of numbers—and the operator on the desk answered, and I told her what had happened, and she said she would send help. And that's the way it was. I don't know whether I was in shock or whether I was just reacting to what had happened. And I think that's why they took me to the hospital on a stretcher because my blood pressure was dropping so low.

Q. And you recall going to the hospital?

A. Yes.

Q. You were conscious?

A. Yes I was conscious. But—and they kept me in another room at the hospital and Tommy in a separate room.

Q. Are you talking about the emergency room?

A. Yes, yes, emergency room. And I feel like we got into our room—into his room, rather, about 12:00 midnight.

Q. What do you recall that you experienced in the way of an examination or treatment at the hospital?

A. Well, they gave me medication—I remember that—two shots or something.

Q. Did they offer to take you back to the motel that night?

A. Yes. The police offered to do, you know, do whatever they could to help me, but I didn't—I wasn't going to leave there.

Q. Why not?

A. I was afraid to. I just couldn't.

Q. What did you observe about Tommy at the hospital, and what was done to him?

A. Well they—they realized he had his jaws broken and that he'd have to stay—be hospitalized—and stay there for the doctor the next morning, and so he did. The next day was the day they operated.

Q. What did he look like after the operation?

A. Well, he was—his mouth was wired together, jaws, and all his teeth, I mean, were wired completely together. But he—after—the next day you could see where he was beaten and bruised.

Q. Was that around his eyes?

A. Yes.

Q. Were they discolored?

A. Well yes, dark and then—yes, and yellow.

Q. How long did Tommy's jaws stay wired shut?

A. I think it was seven weeks.

Q. How long did he stay in the hospital there in North Carolina?

A. Five days, four to five days. From Friday to Tuesday maybe. I stayed in a room with him on a cot.

Q. Did any of your family come down to North Carolina after this?

A. Yes. Our son came down on Saturday, the next day. He came from New York.

Q. And how did you get home?

A. They—well, see, I had the car there. We had a car there, but they took the keys to the car and so I had no key. And I did not go back to the motel; I didn't want to go. The police were kind enough to bring me some things I needed, some clothes and things. And they took me up there on Monday morning to see the room, and to identify some things of mine, and that is when we found out what—they had taken—and I realized they had gone into the trunk of the car that same night. They had used the keys, but we didn't find the keys. Friends came down from Virginia, and brought us more keys to the car.

Q. Who came down for you?

A. Our minister, and several men in the church.

Q. And they brought you all another set of keys?

A. Yes, and some money.

Q. I take it your son drove you back from North Carolina?

A. Yes—my son, and a good friend of ours.

Q. Describe yourself to the jury before February 28, 1981.

A. I was a driving person. I mean, I could—I was not lazy, I would undertake anything that was asked of me, and I enjoyed working with other people and doing things I enjoyed, my work at the store, my church work, club work and things like that.

Q. What kind of club?

A. Well, women's club, a three arts club, garden club.

Q. Between February, 1981, and your heart attack in April, 1982, describe yourself.

A. Well the thing I—when I came—after this incident, I felt

like a person that had been pushed down, and you couldn't get up, like a dog if you tell him to sit and make him stay, like I just couldn't get myself back to my former self. I didn't drive places by myself. When I did leave home to go to work, it was hard to get out of the house and go to the car. I would go to every window to see if anyone was in the yard. I was afraid to get into the car. And when I left the store in the afternoon, I would try to go with one of the employees around back, where we parked. It's hard for me to—the confidence, I haven't regained the confidence I would like to have, as sure of myself.

Q. Tell the jury about your home—the type of security that you had and the locks before and after.

A. We have very good locks on the house, and we added a few other locks. I feel it is a secure house.

Q. What was it like prior to February, 1981?

A. It was left open. At night, we would lock up at night.

Q. But in the daytime you left it unlocked?

A. Yes.

Q. How about now?

A. It's locked. We—we have difficulty hearing people when they come to the front door now, mainly because it is locked.

Q. In your mind do you feel that the assault in Concord had anything to do with your heart attack? [Defense counsel objected to this question; however, Melissa was permitted to answer.]

A. I feel like it did have something to do with it, bound to because of the state I was in and—and that it put me in, which was a buildup of this thing of no confidence in myself, being a person who has been active. And then my work at the store that year before the heart attack—was hard. I made it hard because I wanted to get out of the—this fear I had. And I think that the general buildup probably had something to do with it, but I—because it's on my mind all the time. Every day, there's never been a day I don't think about it, or haven't thought about it, since it happened.

Q. What role did the assault in North Carolina play in the decision to close the business?

A. Mainly what it did to me because I was running the store
   and operating it by myself. And that was a major incident
   that caused us to realize that I wasn't physically able, or
   mentally able, to—to handle it.

Q. What medicines are you taking now?

A. At the moment, I'm taking Restoril, and Xanax.

Q. How do you feel about yourself? [Defense counsel objected
   to this question, but Melissa was permitted to answer.]

A. I feel—when anybody asks me how I feel, I say all right.
   And I feel all right to a point, but I am not emotionally
   stable at all. I don't like people to know that I'm not, but
   I'm not.

Q. All right, I think you've stated that Thomas—your husband
   Thomas—how did he do with this situation. What did you
   observe about him?

A. Well, like he does with situations. He is an unusual person.
   He handles what comes to him, and accepts it. It wasn't
   pleasant, but he did very well with it. But he doesn't—as far
   as the injury was concerned, he accepted it, because he had
   it, and that's what he had to do.

Q. When is your next appointment with [the Doctor]

A. February—February 14,—Valentine's Day.

Q. What do you see going to [the Doctor] has done for you,
   if anything? [Defense counsel objected to this question, but
   Melissa was permitted to answer.]

A. It has helped me definitely. And he's tried—he's tried to
   work with me and advise me what to do in trying to—he
   doesn't get much out of me. I—I—but when I go there, I
   feel better when I leave.

It is nearly impossible to understand such brutal conduct
by one human being toward another. Yet, such deeds occur
nearly every day, under varied circumstances of the nation's
hotel's and motel's.

Melissa and Thomas Butler's experience with sudden violent crime was only a fragment of the security problem that
affected hoteliers in the beautiful foothills of North Carolina,
during 1981. When the Butlers checked into room 109, they had

no reason to suspect that the motels in the area were in the throes of a crime wave directed against motel guests that had commenced in Charlotte, on February 16, 1981. Concord is about a fifteen-minute drive from Charlotte. Three armed subjects assaulted and robbed guests at motels located along Interstate 85 and relatively close to one another.

The local newspapers, as well as the radio and television newscasts were rife with reports of the violence against motel guests by what the media dubbed the "motel bandits" and "motel robbers." The violent attack upon Mr. and Mrs. Butler was but one such attack that served as the Concord connection to the industry's security problems. Each motel guest, victimized by the "motel robbers" was part of a collection of individual human tragedies.

For instance, there was the young couple from Mount Dora, Florida, on their way home with their children after attending a funeral in Laurel, Maryland. They were robbed of their cash and jewelry at gunpoint, but not before their eight year old daughter was forced to watch her mother and father bound hand and foot, and her father repeatedly and brutally kicked by an assailant as he lay helpless upon the motel room floor. The father was quoted in newspaper accounts of this tragedy and described his daughter: "She just can't sleep. She is nervous and fidgety. During the day she is okay. At night, it is another matter." Then there was the man from Rockford, Illinois, at age sixty-six, about the age of Thomas Butler. He was also beaten and robbed of $450 in cash plus an estimated $4,000 in checks and jewelry. Still another gentleman, vice president of a corporation in Chicago, was in Charlotte attending a business convention. Beaten and robbed, he was quoted in the media as saying this about his ordeal "I was gagged with a washcloth pushed down my throat with the barrel of a pistol."

Seven of these sordid crimes occurred prior to the arrival of the Butlers. In all, there were twelve robberies within about a three week period, before the dark cloud passed and the burden was lifted from the people in this beautiful area of North Carolina. It is certain that not all twelve victims of these motel robberies sued the motels where the crimes occurred, but the Butlers did. Their lawsuit revealed that some of the best paid minds in the industry were the authors of chilling chapters from the story of negligence by hotelkeepers.

On the very day Melissa and Thomas Butler arrived in Concord, a local industry trade association had offered a reward of $500 for information leading to the capture of the "motel robbers." That same day, during a meeting among local hoteliers and local law enforcement personnel, a police investigator said that motel robbers are twice as difficult to apprehend, because victims of crimes are passing through and do not plan to stay to study photographs, or otherwise assist in identifying suspects the police may apprehend. There can be no doubt that the transient nature of guests of motels and hotels serves as a major impediment to effective police investigation, as well as the successful prosecution of criminals. Most of the criminals who attack guests know this, just as the police do. It is one reason criminals prey upon motel and hotel guests.

The several law enforcement agencies of the different jurisdictions that were involved in the efforts to apprehend these robbers performed with dedication to duty and cooperated in a professional manner. Their efforts to bring the "motel robbers" to justice reflects favorably upon police work.

According to a five-page Charlotte-Mecklenburg Police Department investigative report, officers from several adjoining jurisdictions assisted in assembling evidence concerning the "motel robbers." Officers developed information through an informant, regarding the identity of one suspect in one of the motel robberies. A sizeable volume of serious crime is solved by information obtained from informers. Information concerning a suspect motor vehicle was obtained by the police investigators and an all-points bulletin was issued. An alert Charlotte police officer on patrol made a suspect vehicle stop in the Five Points area of the city. The car's two occupants were armed and in possession of a number of keys to guest rooms at motels where crimes had occurred. Further police investigation resulted in the arrest of a third suspect in the series of motel robberies.

In a lengthy, ten-page handwritten statement dated March 15, 1981, one of the incarcerated suspects confessed. It was graphic in many details. On one page of the written statement, the suspect stated: "Motels along Interstate 85 are easy to get to and get away fast, that's why we hit or rob some of them."

Several months after this written admission, the "motel robbers" were convicted of the robbery and assault of several motel guests and were sentenced by the court.

The crime scene search technician of the Cabarrus County Sheriff's Department lifted twelve latent prints from items and structural surfaces of guest room 109, including a palm print on the external side of the guest room door. According to a laboratory report, the palm print was identified as that belonging to one of the suspects arrested as the "motel robbers." Unfortunately, however, no one was ever prosecuted or sentenced to a prison term for the brutal attack upon Melissa and Thomas Butler. The prosecutor decided that the public interest would not be advanced by prosecuting the suspects because any sentences connected with a conviction for the Butler assault and robbery would probably run concurrently, not consecutively, for the convictions of crimes committed in other counties, and nearby jurisdictions.

The Holiday Inn in Concord, North Carolina, which served as the crime scene for the attack upon Mr. and Mrs. Butler, was a franchised operation. A few entrepreneurs had formed a company, which in turn operated a number of motels and hotels under a license or franchise agreement with at least two national motel franchisors. Pursuant to the commitment agreement with one of the major franchisors, the company operated the motel franchise in Concord under the registered name and trademark of the national franchisor. The Butlers, therefore, sued the franchisor, franchisee, and the two chief investors in the local company that held the Concord motel franchise.

Soon after the Butlers' attorneys filed the lawsuit, they served the defendant innkeepers with a number of formal written questions, interrogatories, which by legal mandate are answered under oath. Excerpts of the questions and answers to those interrogatories follow:

Q. Admit that the motel could expect a higher incidence of criminal activity at night than during daylight hours.

A. Denied, it being averred that there was no reason to expect criminal activity during night or daylight hours.

Q. State the approximate number of hotels and motels which you owned on February 27, 1981, which were (A) in the U.S., (B) in North Carolina, (C) in the world.

A. On February 27, 1981, 193 in the U.S., 3 in North Carolina and 231 hotels in the world.

Q. Admit that at the time of the assault upon the plaintiffs, the motel had no written security plan or protocol located on the premises concerning guest security.

A. It is admitted that there was no such written plan or protocol.

Q. State what measures were taken prior to the night of February 27, 1981, to increase security in response to the activities of the "motel robbers."

A. Do not know of any group known as "motel robbers," in the Concord area, and there was no reason to believe increased security was warranted at the motel.

According to the North Carolina Department of Justice Uniform Crime Report for Cabarrus County, where Concord is located, the county experienced 153 aggravated assaults, and 40 robberies during 1979. On January 20th of that year, one of those armed robberies was committed at the motel in Concord. Apparently armed robbery was not unknown in the placid rural county of Cabarrus, nor unknown at the motel located there.

Totally eclipsing these facts, however, is the revelation that the Concord motel was associated with two motels in Charlotte where motel guests were also victimized by the "motel robbers." The manager of one of the affiliate Charlotte motels was, in fact, the president of the local industry trade association responsible for offering the $500 for the capture of the "motel robbers."

A preponderance of evidence existed that danger and the possibility of harm to the guests was present at the motel immediately prior to Mr. and Mrs. Butler's arrival in Concord. Despite this, no motel employee informed them of the danger when they arrived. Informing the guests would have alerted them to take precautions to protect themselves against possible violent, criminal attack. Not only was this not done, but the motel chose to check them into an isolated area of the premises where virtually no other guests were roomed. Melissa Butler saw no other automobiles where her husband parked their car because it was an isolated area, out of sight from the front desk office. It was an area with unimpeded access from several directions, both by vehicle and on foot. Owing to a normal low occupancy on weekends, the motel could logically and easily have roomed the two senior citizens close to the front desk office area. The crime of armed robbery is enhanced by isolation because there is an absence of witnesses to interrupt the crime or serve as aides to police investigation. As hoteliers who hold themselves up to the public as professionals, through their nationally recognized trademarks, the motel should have known this. After all, professionals are held to a higher standard of conduct than non-professionals, and rightly so.

The geographical location of the motel, just a few yards away from two major highway systems, was not without potential serious security problems. This was especially true, since the motel provided no viable perimeter protection to deter and reduce the incidence of criminal trespass. The two highway systems close to the motel permitted circumstances that facilitated a quick escape by assailants.

An assistant manager of the motel gave testimony in this case that proved most unfavorable to the motel. In court and under oath, few employees will offer perjured testimony for their employer. This motel manager testified that the activities of the "motel robbers" were common knowledge among motel employees, untrained by management in matters regarding guest security. He also stated that some employees expressed fear for their own safety. This assistant manager further testified that prior to the attack on the Butlers, he contacted his supervisor in Charlotte. This man turned out to be the same manager who served as president of the local trade association. The assistant manager of the Holiday Inn had asked for approval to hire security officers on an interim basis, until the "motel robbers" were apprehended. But he was told that expenses incurred in providing security were unwarranted. He was told to do the best he could; that no additional operating money would be provided. According to the evidence in this case, gross income for the Concord motel was $432,856.62.

Well into the litigation of this case, the motel's legal team attempted to change the increasing perception that the innkeeper was careless and indifferent toward the security of his guests by offering the testimony of an expert security witness. This "expert", however, had never worked in any hotel or motel in a security capacity. Ultimately, the man never testified at the trial, although his pre-trial sworn testimony is part of the case record. One of the chief thrusts of his testimony dealt with his belief that the motel exercised reasonable care for guest security by encouraging local law enforcement personnel to frequent the premises. He contended that this was a part of guest security and that if police presence on the premises did not deter the "motel robbers," hiring security officers certainly would not. This is a line of testimony often offered by defense counsel "expert" witnesses who provide testimony for the defense of hoteliers faced with guest security-related litigation. It sounds good. But under careful scrutiny, such testimony is invariably revealed to be untenable. In this case, law enforcement officers testified at trial that they did in fact patronize the dining room of the motel, but that such visits were infrequent. At the time of the attack on the Butlers, no law enforcement officers were on the premises. They further testified that while seated inside the motel dining room, their view of the motel guest rooms was obstructed and seriously limited. The presence of law enforcement officers accomplishes nothing, unless they are first observed by those planning to commit crime. Therefore, patrol stops have a very limited deterrent effect upon crime within the innkeeping environment.

Public law enforcement departments are often understaffed, and therefore overworked. The public owes a debt of gratitude to law enforcement personnel. Their work is often dangerous and difficult. Everyone benefits from the efforts and dedication of the police. The public sector law enforcement effort is the cement of our social structure, holding society together against the terrible torrent of criminal forces at work to destroy social order, peace and harmony. Law enforcement officers, however, exist in addition to the citizen—not instead of the citizen—to maintain law and social order. The practice of diverting public sector law enforcement efforts from the public to the private sector, is strictly self-serving. This is often done in lieu of employing private security. It removes resources from the public sector, diminishing the effectiveness of an already over-burdened police effort. Such conduct by hotelkeepers contributes little to community crime fighting efforts and serves strictly penurious and private interests.

Approximately five years after the violent attack upon Melissa and Thomas Butler in Concord, North Carolina, the couple had their day in court. In September of 1986, the civil trial pitting the Butlers against the motel, was heard before a jury in the U.S. District Court for the Middle District of North Carolina. In the middle of the one-week trial, Melissa and Thomas Butler, their eldest son, their expert witness and their two attorneys, were assembled in a witness room, located just a few feet down the hall from the courtroom. Witness rooms are often rather stark places, with white paint and austere, stark furniture. The immaculate condition of the witness room of this old court building, somehow added to the sterile atmosphere.

The younger of the two attorneys spoke first. He began to explain to his clients, and their son, that there had been a turn of events in their case. He went on to explain that the defense counsel representing the defendant motel had now expressed a willingness to settle the case, by meeting the pre-trial settlement demand, which was in six figures. The animated attorney explained that it was now a matter for the Butlers to consider, and to decide either to accept it, or to continue with the trial. Both attorneys were men of integrity and neither sought to influence the decision of their clients.

Thomas Butler listened carefully to every word. When the attorneys finished their explanation, Thomas glanced at his wife Melissa, and their eyes met briefly. Then he focused squarely and clearly as he began to speak. "We did not do this for the money. It is a matter of principle. It is a matter of principle to us. Let's proceed with the trial, and let the jury decide." Within a short time, the federal jury did decide. It awarded Melissa Butler $400,000 in compensatory damages, and her beloved husband of nearly half a century was awarded $100,000.

As expected, the defendant's legal team sought an appeal of the decision through post-verdict motions on a variety of legal issues. In October 1987 the case was argued before the U.S. Court of Appeals, and the following April, the three-judge appellate court upheld the jury award of the trial court. Two judges affirmed, and one judge filed a concurring and dissenting opinion. The dissenting member of the court concurred with the majority opinion regarding the security aspects of the case. He stated: "The assault upon the plaintiffs was absolutely dreadful." His dissent addressed the legal issue of the link between the assault and Melissa's heart attack fourteen months after the criminal assault.

It should be recalled that the lawsuit against the motel was directed against several defendants, including the local franchisee as well as the national franchisor. This case was somewhat unique because the national franchisor was kept in the case throughout the trial. In many instances, industry corporations that franchise their corporate names to independent operators are dismissed from liability.

Excerpts of the decision of the U.S. Court of Appeals, Fourth District, follows:

> By virtue of the franchise agreement, the franchisor retained a significant degree of control over the operation of the franchisee motel in Concord. This control included the use of the franchisor name, and trademarks, which appeared on numerous items in and about the motel premises. The company engages in national advertising that promotes its national system, without distinguishing between company owned, and franchised properties. We think that a jury could reasonably conclude that the motel in Concord, North Caro-

lina, was operated in such a way as to create the appearance that it was owned by the company franchisor, and that this was one of the purposes of the franchise agreement.

To prove that the special duty of care created by the circumstances was breached, the Butlers relied primarily upon the testimony of an expert in hotel and motel security.

The defendants also attempted to portray the motel as a quiet, safe motel, that did not require the extreme security measures urged by [the security expert].

In the two weeks just before the attack on the Butlers, seven motels within the general area had been victimized by what the police and press identified as the same group of assailants.

Finally, the evidence is sufficient to establish that it was reasonably foreseeable that the Concord motel might be a target.

Considering the security expert's testimony, and the fact the franchisor's own loss prevention manual suggests some of the same security measures whose absence is emphasized, we think there was enough evidence for the jury to reasonably conclude the defendants breached their duty to provide adequate security to protect their guests against the specific known foreseeable risk created by the circumstances.

The jury was entitled to accept the innkeeping security expert's opinions that criminals typically assess the risk of apprehension presented by security measures in place, frequently by on site surveillance of the premises, and that the measures taken on the premises here in issue would not act as an effective deterrent.

That relatively lax security measures necessarily enhance the attractiveness of a particular motel as a potential target, is manifest.

Having accepted this conclusion, the jury could reasonably have inferred—though surely it need not have—that the Butlers' assailants were indeed emboldened by the lax security measures, to come on the premises, size up the situation, and plan their assault.

The motel continued its program to encourage local law enforcement personnel to frequent the premises by offering free snack trays, and discount meals in the restaurant, though it did not employ any as security guards.

Looking first to Melissa Butler, the jury awarded her four hundred thousand dollars in compensatory damages. The evidence at trial was sufficient for the jury to conclude that she has been deeply affected by the incident both physically and emotionally, and that she has not yet recovered. Her psychiatrist testified that she suffers from severe mental disorders as a result of the assault, and will not likely return to her former self. Her medical costs alone amounted to over forty thousand dollars. During the ordeal, she was threatened with death, a gun was placed to her head, and she was bound and gagged. She twice witnessed the beating of her husband, and at one point was lead to believe he was dead.

As for Thomas Butler, the jury awarded him one hundred thousand dollars compensatory damages. The evidence at trial showed he had been beaten severely and had his jaw broken in two places. His jaw was wired closed for six weeks. Though he has fully recovered from this incident, his life has been dramatically altered as a result of the assault and its aftermath.

The grant or denial of a motion for a new trial on the ground that the verdict is excessive, is a matter committed to the sound discretion of the trial court. We may not reverse denial of the motion unless the verdict is untoward, inordinate, unreasonable, or outrageous'.

These awards are not outrageous in light of the evidence which the jury was entitled to accept. We thus decline to set them aside.

This Appeals Court decision is merely one of many such decisions that have reinforced trial court awards against members of the innkeeping industry and that have served to sustain a strict standard of penalty for many hotelkeepers whose negligent conduct is evident.

Innkeeping Personnel and Security

The end of World War II in 1945 ushered in an era of unprecedented economic growth and increased individual prosperity for most Americans. This resulted in vast commercial expansion and the acquisition of personal wealth.

Impressive improvements in public transportation, specifically air travel, as well as expansion and improvement of the nation's highway systems permitted enhanced mobility. These circumstances, along with increased private automobile ownership, have resulted in a mushrooming of business and leisure travel. Overnight, the country seemed magically transformed into a smaller place as Americans became avid travelers. As a natural result of these new conditions, a rapid growth and expansion of the market for innkeeping services developed. Through successful national advertising, innkeeping became glamorous and exciting. Innkeepers were provided the opportunity to develop and the challenge to grow.

Developers, investors, and hotel-motel operators responded quickly to the varied economic, social, and environmental requirements of an ever rapidly growing number of traveling Americans. A few hoteliers developed into major national and regional innkeeping chains, becoming household names. It was during this era that the acronym motel, derived from the words motoring and hotel, became a neologism.

This dynamic industry growth created an enormous demand for labor, that resulted in a great influx of both skilled and unskilled workers into the work force of hotels and motels across the nation. The vocational training of vast numbers of workers throughout the rapidly expanding industry became a major challenge confronting hoteliers. Ostensibly, the industry responded to this challenge by adopting on-the-job training methods, whereby an employee already on the job trains a new hire. This method of training new industry employees was adopted to the almost complete exclusion of other methods of instruction such as classroom instruction. On-the-job training continues to enjoy widespread industry use, and only a small number of industry personnel receive training and instruction by qualified professionals, who use recognized authoritative sources of educational material.

Some of the major innkeeping chains have developed various courses of instruction for their employees. Such courses, almost always offered within the hotel or motel, are of short duration and attended on a voluntary basis. Unfortunately, the high attrition rate among industry employees has a debilitating effect on educational efforts. According to the 1977 U.S. Government report entitled "Crime in Service Industries," the annual turnover rate among industry personnel frequently exceeds 70%. There is no reason to expect this percentage to have appreciably diminished since 1977. Such an attrition rate certainly is not conducive to an atmosphere of learning.

Several of the nation's finest universities offer four-year, degree courses in hotel administration. Concerning the central issue of the security of guests within the hotel or motel environment, the academic community has mimicked hotelkeepers in its response to the growing menace of violent crime. For years, colleges of hotel administration have skirted the issue of guest security by offering their students courses concerning innkeeping law, not guest security. Industry law only remotely addresses guest security. As recently as 1988, one of the nation's most respected colleges of hotel administration, Cornell University, offered a curriculum requiring only one semester of "law and hotel administration" for graduation. Since the innkeeping industry supports colleges offering degrees in hotel administration through grants, scholarships and endowments and holds widespread influence, industry leaders must share the responsibility for this appalling situation.

While on-the-job training became increasingly in vogue among hoteliers as a means of training innkeeping personnel, it also became evident such training was inadequate in providing conditions favorable for exercising reasonable security for the guest. The reason this training method failed in this regard is simple. Employees who instruct others in matters bearing on guest security ordinarily do not offer instruction based on firsthand experience—but only on their own employee to employee education. Thus, the mainstay of innkeeping training is based purely on hearsay. The discipline of innkeeping security is by no means secret, yet it is a specialized discipline of knowledge. Hearsay instruction in guest security, is as effective as hearsay instruction in driving an automobile. Obviously, it is a reckless practice that can lead to disastrous results. The employee encounter with this condition is seminal. Valid and effective guest security measures become obscured, distorted and even lost altogether.

While industry reliance upon on-the-job instruction perpetuates flawed knowledge, it also insidiously erodes the collective industry awareness of the hotelkeepers' legal duties to exercise reasonable care for their guests through the sound practice of security methods.

The twin misconceptions of innkeeping security, popular to staff personnel, are the belief it can do everything and the belief that it can do nothing. Within the spectrum of these two opposite beliefs fall the varying degrees of guest security practices by industry management. Within the present atmosphere of epidemic violent crime in American society, most innkeeping establishments like the Concord, North Carolina, motel property have no established written policy in place for providing guest security.

Within the industry, ongoing guest security policies are most likely to be in place only in the major chains. Even here, such policies are found to exist in varying degrees. Large properties, most often in major cities, often provide a department of security headed by a director and staffed with security personnel. Smaller properties within these chains then, may, or may not, provide security personnel.

At the corporate level, some, but not all, national and regional hotel chains employ a corporate director of security on their staff. It has recently become popular to retain risk managers. Unfortunately, very few of these major hotels provide middle level security management.

Directors of security at either the property or corporate level are ostensibly administrators with manifold duties and responsibilities. But, no duty can supersede the duty to protect employees and the public from violent criminal attack. Where employed, corporate directors of security commonly oversee the security operations of fifty or more subordinates. And at the property level, directors often supervise fifteen to thirty security officers. This responsibility is not trivial. For instructional purposes and comparison, the U.S. Bureau of Statistics provides recent information illustrating that nearly half of the nation's public law enforcement agencies employ fewer than ten officers; 79% fewer than twenty-five sworn officers.

Like their subordinates, most industry directors of security are undertrained and often underpaid. Unfortunately, the industry community of security personnel is not immune from the ravages of high attrition rates. Security personnel are infrequently paid at a rate reflecting the trust, responsibility, and dangers associated with their work. In this regard, their renumeration differs little from that of public law enforcement officers.

In the infrequent instance where members of the industry do in fact retain directors of security, management typically hires former or retired law enforcement personnel, neither knowledgeable, nor experienced in innkeeping operations, or the discipline of innkeeping security. This inveterate condition is wasteful because it fails to use personnel with firsthand experience. And worse, it contributes directly to the high attrition rate among innkeeping security personnel. In addition to its other shortcomings, this longstanding practice fails to reward the hard work and loyalty of security personnel by failing to promote from within their ranks.

The link in this system is obscure, but nevertheless cannot be ignored. This link is the connection between the longstanding system of a "good ole boy" network. Public law enforcement personnel, nearing retirement or retired, are frequently hired by hoteliers as the result of casual friendships forged from occasional professional contact. Since public sector law enforcement and private sector security are separate disciplines, experience in one of them does not automatically qualify anyone for work in the related field. No one without appropriate credentials should claim that which the title director of security implies.

Innkeeping security knowledge is at a premium because industry management has failed to provide credible education and on-the-job training for its security personnel, in general, and its directors in particular. Directors of security are trained the same way as other industry employees, chiefly through the questionable methods mentioned earlier. Knowledge acquired in this way predisposes the unlearned director to error in the application of viable security methods in protecting the public.

At the corporate level of operations, on-the-job training of a director of security takes a slight twist. This director is almost immediately dispatched into the corporation's field operations to visit individual corporate hotel or motel properties. In theory, the unlearned director is sent to ask questions about security practices at the property for the purpose of review and evaluation. This usually produces a written survey of the premises visited. In truth, the unlearned director is unqualified by background and experience to conduct such a security evaluation. In reality, this is a well orchestrated ruse by corporate superiors to educate the neophyte director through the opportunity to consult with, and "pick the brains" of security personnel at the property level.

In terms of credibility, this training method has little value, since those who would instruct often possess little knowledge beyond their student's. This lamentable situation exists because of the high industry attrition rate. Veteran security personnel, knowledgeable enough to instruct, are scarce in number.

Directors of security hired from outside the industry's ranks are faced with two foremost challenges. First, they must learn about innkeeping operations in general, and second, they must learn about innkeeping security in particular. In practical terms, directors of security at either the property or corporate level are powerless to effect true changes except those made through the art of persuading and influencing executive management. Directors serve as advisors and counselors to their corporate superiors regarding security matters. Ordinarily they possess no power to appropriate funds for capital improvements, employee training or labor costs; all associated with guest security. As advisors, these security directors have been ill prepared by their superiors for their work. This situation is widespread throughout the industry, and often results in danger to the public and in turn to more problems in terms of the ongoing dilemma over guest security.

There has been a marked evaporation of industry career loyalty among security personnel. A sizeable segment of the archaic management within the industry maintains the concept of employee expendability. This antiquated management style fosters an employment system of wages and benefits deceptively designed to reward long-term tenure, while the industry attrition rate does not justify such a system of renumeration.

It is by no means abnormal that guests should maintain a high expectation for the professional training of industry security personnel. The absence of such training is the fault of both the ordinary innkeeper and the ordinary industry manager, who place profit before devotion to their guests' safety.

For instance, there is the case of an airline stewardess who was a registered guest of a large hotel. Upon checking in, she went directly to her room, but she left the door ajar because she was momentarily awaiting the arrival of another stewardess. They planned to make arrangements to socialize and dine together. An armed intruder entered the guest room. He closed and locked the door behind him and then robbed the hotel guest of her cash. The hotel employed one security officer, on duty at the time of this attack. Although he immediately responded to the guest room when notified of the assault, the assailant escaped capture. The stewardess subsequently filed a lawsuit against the hotel, claiming that one security officer could not provide reasonable security for all the guests. In response, the hotel pulled an old concept out of the hotel closet. It claimed that guest security is the responsibility of all employees, making all the employees of the hotel participants in the security function. This is a standard defense resurrected from a long dormant concept.

At the time of the assault upon the stewardess, there were

approximately 70 housekeeping personnel on duty, as well as engineers, bellmen, and room service personnel. The hotel claimed that all of these employees were performing their basic work skills, and were also involved in the hotel security function of providing reasonable care for guests.

Hotel employees, called to testify before the trial jury claimed that they had never received any training in guest security. In fact, no one had ever discussed guest security with them and no one in management had ever explained to them that they were expected to perform their ordinary work and also to participate in the hotel security effort by asking guests to keep their room doors closed and locked.

A trial jury awarded the stewardess nearly seventy-five thousand dollars, almost double the amount the plaintiff's attorney had demanded in settlement prior to the trial. In addition, the contract with this hotel to regularly provide lodging for airline personnel was terminated.

A Familiar Problem

The importance of appropriate security staffing and training becomes increasingly apparent as newspapers continue to chronicle violent crime across the country.

During the spring of 1993, public attention was focused on "tourist robberies" in South Florida. The *Miami Herald* reported that robberies of out-of-state vacationers rose from 1,165 in 1989 to 2,616 in 1992. In Miami alone, in 1991, these robberies more than doubled in a two-month period, from 80 in September to 163 in November. Of course, not all of the so called "tourist robberies" occurred on hotel or motel properties, but many did.

For instance, in March 1993, a German tourist was killed by a robber outside his Days Inn motel room in Homestead. A multi-million dollar lawsuit has already been filed in this case.

While these violent attacks underscore widespread industry security problems, they are neither unusual nor unfamiliar. Another story reported in the *Miami Herald* was about a Scranton couple, who were beaten and robbed inside their room in a North Dade Holiday Inn. Their attorney disclosed that this vicious assault was the thirty-seventh crime reported at the motel during a twelve-month period. The robbers were inside the couple's room when they entered. The man was pistol-whipped and his injuries required five operations. He was permanently disabled. His wife, also beaten, suffered severe psychological damage. The couple's lawsuit was settled out-of-court for $800,000. But you won't find the story of this case in any recent edition of the *Miami Herald*. It occurred on the afternoon of November 11, 1975.

In response to the media attention to South Florida's "tourist robberies," David L. Edgell, Undersecretary of Commerce for Travel and Tourism issued the following statement:

"We are encouraged by the proactive response of the State of Florida that all measures possible are being undertaken to insure the security and safety of all visitors. And it is important to bear in mind that America remains one of the safest places in the world to visit and enjoy."

In contrast, Klaus Sommer, Germany's Consul-General in Miami reportedly stated to journalists:

"The increase of physical injury and killing is getting much higher than any comparable civilized place around the world...This is horrible. My patience has come to an end."

The Commerce Department's U.S. Travel and Tourism Administration (USTTA) works closely with travel industry suppliers, including hotelkeepers, to promote domestic and foreign travel. AH&MA's Government Affairs Committee marshalled support for the 1980 National Tourism Policy Act. This Act of Congress established the USTTA to replace the old U.S. Travel Service and elevated its status with the designation of an Under Secretary of Commerce.

It is disconcerting that USTTA spends taxpayer dollars to assist the innkeeping industry and yet has not developed and implemented any requirements for the security of guests as a test for its continued promotion. This is despite the fact that, as far back as its September 1977 report, the U.S. Department of Commerce acknowledged the industry's serious guest security problems.

While the idea is promoted that the traveling public is safer today, more guests are being injured and killed. And it should be recognized that of the "tourist robberies" that occur on hotel and motel properties, the statistics only represent reported crimes. As the number of crimes against travelers continues to rise, a state like Florida, whose lifeblood is an estimated 30 billion dollar tourism industry, is seriously threatened, along with millions in profits for its hotelkeepers.

Three

Certain Key Concerns

It was nearly 2:00 a.m. Central Standard Time, as the teenager walked briskly across the nearly empty hotel lobby toward the guest elevators. Susan Holway was tired. It had been a long day of activity, and she was anxious to get some sleep before she would have to rise and catch the charter bus back to her college campus. As she stepped inside the elevator car, two airline pilots greeted her, and she scarcely noticed the well-dressed man with the briefcase, who slipped in right behind her.

Susan pressed the elevator panel button for the tenth floor. During the brief, smooth ride up, the pilots made some small talk, mentioning how tired they were after a long flight. Upon arrival on the tenth floor, the elevator came to a quiet stop and the doors quickly parted. Susan bade the pilots goodnight, as the man with the briefcase preceded her alighting from the car. The man purposely hesitated as Susan passed him by, and the pilots disappeared behind the closing doors.

The old hotel was very large and considered by many to be a city landmark. Susan's guest room was located some distance from the tenth floor elevator foyer. Because of the hour, the corridor and adjoining hallways were very quiet, and no one was present except the teenager and the man who had ridden up on the elevator with her.

As Susan Holway walked toward her room, she sensed the man behind her. She quickened her pace. After passing a number of rooms, Susan continued to hear the light sound of the man's footsteps in the soft carpet behind her. The sounds came closer and closer as the man shortened the distance between them. Soon, all Susan could hear was his footsteps and the pounding of her heart. Walking very quickly now, Susan placed her hand inside her shoulder purse in search of her guest room key. In doing this, she found the small canister of chemical spray she always carried with her, and this provided a sense of comfort to her. Suddenly, the man was beside her and without warning reached out with one arm, and grabbed the startled young woman around the neck. As she resisted the man's assault, Susan cried out for help. She screamed repeatedly. Remaining on her feet, she struggled with her assailant and pulled the chemical spray from her purse. With courage and determination, Susan discharged the chemical into the face of her assailant, as she continued to cry out for help. Unfortunately, her defensive action failed to deter the attack. The assailant wrestled Susan to the floor. For what seemed an eternity, she resisted her attacker until finally he placed his hand on her throat, and began to slowly choke her. With a smirk on his face, he assured her that no one was going to help her. Sadly, he was correct. He told the teenage guest that if she did not cease resisting, he was going to put her "asleep for a long time." She was close to losing consciousness when he released his grip on her throat. Then he dragged Susan to a nearby room, removed a guest key from his pocket, and used the key to enter. Forced inside, Susan was terrified, exhausted and in pain. During the next 45 minutes or so, the young college student was raped and sodomized. As Susan's assailant prepared to leave the room, he warned his victim not to try leaving for a long time. Pretending to leave the room, he remained silent, lurking in the shadow against the wall. Susan did not move because she was able to see her attacker through a full-length mirror on a closet door. After a minute had elapsed, the assailant walked back to the terrified teenager, and with an arrogance often characteristic of a sociopath, told her he was just testing her and that he had many tricks up his sleeve. He again warned his victim about trying to leave the guest room. At this point, he departed the room, and was never seen again.

After her assailant departed, the young victim ran to the door and engaged the security chain. There was no way for Susan to dead-bolt the guest room door, because the unsafe and antiquated hotel lock required the guest, while inside the room, to insert the room key into the lock to activate the dead-bolt. Susan did not have the room key; the criminal had it.

Next, Susan called a fellow member of the student tour group on the guest room telephone. She asked her friend to come to the room and to help her. Within minutes, two friends arrived. They tried to comfort Susan and walked her back to their own room. Once safely inside, she explained what had happened and took a nice warm shower to feel clean again. However, by doing this she unwittingly destroyed evidence. Susan's friends encouraged her to report the crime, but she was reluctant. She feared becoming the topic of conversation among students in the tour. She shared the perception of public stigma often experienced by victims of rape. Finally, a long distance conversation in the early morning hours with Susan's older sister persuaded the young victim to report the crime and her friends placed a call to the hotel operator, who in turn notified the hotel security office of the guest complaint.

Nearly ten stories below the hotel floor where Susan was viciously attacked, the night manager sat placidly in the lobby office of the assistant manager. This particular night manager had been employed by the major hotel chain for about twelve years and at the time of the attack upon Susan Holway, he was working part-time on weekends. Once notified by the security office of the guest's complaint, the night manager assembled several members of the hotel security department and went directly to the crime scene. (Why the hotel employees responded to this room, and not to the room where the complainant awaited them, remains somewhat of a mystery.) The contingent of hotel employees found no one, although there was evidence that the room had been used. Hotel personnel determined that the room was not registered to any guest, and hotel records showed the room vacant and unoccupied. Thinking that the housekeeping department had failed to clean and prepare the room upon the departure of a previous registered guest and that the complaint received was invalid, the night manager and security personnel left the tenth floor and resumed their normal duties. No further investigation was conducted by hotel personnel at this time, although the nature of the complaint was most serious.

After patiently awaiting a hotel response to their initial call, Susan's friends called the telephone operator a second time. About 45 minutes had elapsed between the first and second calls for help. In response to this second call, the night manager and one security department staffer reported to the room where Susan and her friends anxiously awaited.

By now, almost two full hours had passed since the stranger had assaulted Susan Holway in the tenth floor corridor. While interviewing Susan, and as she described the sordid details of her hotel nightmare, the security officer reached into his suit pocket and removed a small canister of chemical spray, which Susan immediately identified. The night manager would later state in a sworn deposition that the weapon had been discovered in the tenth floor corridor by a security patrol officer, during security's response to the call from Susan's friends. But this explanation was inconsistent with other sworn testimony. For instance, the security patrol officer later reported that he actually had found the chemical spray weapon, as well as a woman's hair barrette, about an hour before anyone else had responded to a call about the tenth-floor crime. This officer also stated that he had responded to a tenth-floor guest complaint about noise, and at that time found the chemical spray weapon and barrette. He thought them suspicious and took the items to the night manager. The night manager dismissed the items, as well as the circumstances, as meaningless. This security officer next turned the items over to the security office, where, according to security operating procedures, the items should have been recorded in a log book. However, they were never recorded. The testimony of a hotel guest lent credibility to the statement made by the security patrol officer. This testimony, by a woman who occupied a room on the tenth floor, stated that she had heard repeated cries for help and what sounded like a violent altercation taking place in the corridor outside her room. She said that she had feared opening her door and called the hotel telephone operator two or three times, but the line was busy. Finally, she got through and reported a woman was screaming for help. She furnished her name and room number to the hotel operator, and had waited, in vain, for hotel personnel to contact her concerning her complaint. This guest established the time of her call as the same time as the attack on Ms. Holway.

According to a police report titled *Area One Violent Crimes Detective Division*, Ms. Holway stated that she would have to think about returning to the city in order to view photographs of suspects and she was too upset during the police interview to make such a decision. In virtually all crimes of violence committed against guests, the problem of the transient nature of the victim surfaces. The law enforcement community knows this, and obviously predators of hotel-motel guests understand it. This condition retards arrest rates and increases the success rate of criminals. The police investigating this violent crime attempted to bring the perpetrator to justice. Unfortunately, no one has ever been arrested, or charged with the crime committed against Ms. Holway.

The hotel that became the scene for the attack upon the teenage guest was no "mom and pop" operation, by any stretch of the imagination. It was a hotel that was operated by an elite national hotel chain, regarded as an innkeeping industry leader, and trusted by the public. The founder of this major chain is regarded as an icon; his name has become and remains, a household word to millions of Americans.

This case is indicative of conduct by far too many industry leaders. On the one hand, a character of corporate conduct provides hotel guests with an opulent level of service which often includes room service with fresh flowers, and a nightly turndown with imported chocolates conspicuously placed on the guest room pillows. On the other hand, an entirely different character of corporate conduct concerning public safety often results in nightmares for the guest. Some of the most successful, prominent and influential members of the industry, are at the same time prominent contributors to the industry's security problems. These problems are amplified by the cornucopia of legal evidence revealed through guest security-related litigation.

In 1984, Ms. Holway's attorneys filed a major lawsuit

against the hotel where she was attacked. The evidence of negligent conduct reached deep inside the offices of senior corporate executives of this giant innkeeping chain. This is not inconsistent with the failures that can be extrapolated from the guest security dilemma. The Holway lawsuit furnished an unusual amount of pre-trial evidence—cardboard boxes full of reports, diagrams, documents, and transcripts of sworn testimony. The transcript testimony of the hotel director of security alone, covered three days of oral examination and produced three volumes, totalling over four hundred pages. Buried deep within this generous number of court documents is a revealing narrative of negligent security policies and practices by hotel management personnel and their subordinates. It is corroborated by evidentiary documentation that in some instances was obtained by court order.

It is not surprising that the hotel director of security was a retired state police officer who had already served the public for twenty-seven years. (As stated earlier, innkeeping management has a propensity for hiring security directors from police ranks, outside the industry.) When hired, the gentleman knew little about the business of innkeeping—even less about innkeeping guest security. This hotel offered roughly 1,000 rooms to the public, but it did little to prepare the neophyte director for the awesome responsibility of overseeing 1,000 rooms. On-the-job training was the chief method of instruction. In 1980, this director attended a one-week security conference held in Colorado, under the auspices of the corporate security department. At the time of his testimony, he had left the hotel chain and had obtained a security position outside the industry.

At the time of Ms. Holway's ordeal, the hotel security department was authorized to have thirty staff members and a secretary. Security officers were encouraged to attend, on a voluntary basis, courses related to their work. This is often done so hotels don't have to pay overtime. But, no formal training in security was required, and new security personnel were trained by hotel management through the method of on-the-job training, augmented by corporate manuals on security policy.

During the early morning hours of the criminal assault on Ms. Holway, the security department was operating with two fewer security officers than authorized. In practical terms, this meant that security officers assigned to patrol the guest floors were automatically assigned additional floors to patrol, and this naturally resulted in the reduced frequency of patrolling each floor. This situation also suggests an increase in the time required to respond to the scene of reported security problems.

The hotel guest security conditions described thus far do not reflect the exercise of reasonable care for the public's safety. But, these dangers to public safety pale when compared to the overwhelming negligence connected with Susan Holway's lawsuit—the breach of the security of guest room keys, directly resulting in the use of a vacant hotel room by a trespasser for the commission of a felony. Whenever a hotel or motel of any size loses control of the keys to its rooms, the locks become obsolete. The evidence in this lawsuit proves that the security of the guest room keys at this hotel was seriously breached, and this rendered the locks useless.

Hundreds of this particular hotel's security incident reports were rife with narratives of criminal trespassers on the guest room floors at all hours of the day and night. The passive security posture of hotel management actually encouraged this activity. In documented incidents, trespassers were discovered in rooms, then simply asked to leave the premises. These security reports reveal that room keys were often recovered from underneath fire extinguishers located throughout the guest room corridors. Master keys were missing and unauthorized employees frequently possessed these keys. During inspections of employees' lockers, room keys were found. In addition, on each guest floor throughout the hotel, management had installed key box receptacles at elevator foyers to facilitate the return of room keys by the guests. They remained in place for several months until it was discovered that they were not secure—that anyone could gain entry and remove any number of deposited guest room keys. Two room key receptacles were also placed at the front desk reception area and were left unlocked, providing access to the hotel's rooms. Each key clearly indicated the guest room lock it opened, because hotel management made certain the room number was engraved into the key. Whenever the front desk ran low on room keys, an order was sent to the engineering department locksmith, who dutifully ground out more keys for the front desk. No questions were asked about missing keys. With such an overt breach in the security of room keys, it takes no genius to grasp how easily Ms. Holway's assailant may have acquired a number of guest room keys.

According to the industry's rule of thumb, a given hotel or motel will lose one guest room key per month for each guest room. The circumstances of reasonable care concerning the control of guest room keys by management certainly did not exist at this hotel. Devastating too, is evidence that corporate senior executives were put on notice of numerous serious breaches of guest security at this hotel, long before the teenage college student was criminally assaulted. This evidence surfaced in a copy of correspondence from the corporate director of security to the general manager of the hotel. This four-page correspondence was written one year, three months, and ten days prior to the attack on Ms. Holway. Copies of the correspondence were distributed to the directors' superiors, who included senior corporate executives. This corporate correspondence had been written as a follow-up to a security survey of the hotel by the corporate security director. It recommended action be taken concerning certain practices. On page two, the director mentions the fact that the guest room locks had been in place for approximately 55 years. Using the industry's rule of thumb— the ratio of one lost key per month for each guest room, this hotel property of over one thousand rooms lost, by conservative estimate, over 600,000 room keys.

These conditions are a serious breach of public trust, and suggest corporate negligence. It further demonstrates a blatant and arrogant disregard for the safety of hotel guests. Logically, such conduct gives rise to legitimate concern for the guest security policies and practices of the less affluent, less successful, and less prestigious hoteliers. That such guest security conditions flourished and thrived within the operations of an elite national chain and were tolerated within the highest levels of corporate management is scandalous.

This self-insured innkeeping giant agreed to an out-of-court settlement long before the trial date. When a pattern of negligence becomes evident during the pre-trial development of a case, the negligent hotelkeeper abandons any lofty idea of courtroom victory. Hotelkeepers avidly seek to avoid a public trial, because lawsuits are their nemesis. Out-of-court settlements provide the perfect vehicle for them to hide their conduct from the arena of public scrutiny—the courtroom. In this way, public disclosure of evidence of the industry's widespread negligence can be successfully hidden by those most responsible for allowing the problem to exist.

To return to an earlier case, within months after the Connie Francis case, a widely respected industry leader, president of then Western International Hotels, declared that security had historically been a major concern of industry members. He noted that during the 1970's, security would probably rival energy conservation as the chief concern of hoteliers. He also acknowledged that judges were awarding surprisingly large damage amounts to industry guests who became victims of violent crime. But, the statements of concern for guest security by a few industry leaders belied actual industry measures taken on behalf of patrons. Innkeeping industry managers continued to install unsafe locks in thousands of guest rooms, many of which are still in use today. Unsafe guest security conditions then existed, and continue to exist. This is cause for great concern. This situation is exacerbated by evidence that some hotelkeepers choose not to correct negligent security conditions even when such conditions are known by them to exist.

On a hot Fourth of July, a twenty-six year old woman was beaten, robbed and assaulted, while registered as a guest of a California motel. This motel was operated under a license agreement with a national hotel franchisor. The two assailants were never arrested or prosecuted for their crime. The victim filed a lawsuit against the motel, alleging that the lock on her guest room door was inadequate, and therefore, unsafe. The victim also alleged that the motel had failed to provide adequate security patrols upon the premises to deter this criminal attack. In response, the motel countered that the lock was adequate, and disputed the victim's claim that she was actually raped. Surprisingly, this is often a position taken by a hotel or motel when sued for a crime involving sexual assault. During pre-trial negotiations, the motel offered $10,000 to settle the lawsuit, but later reduced this figure to $5,000. The victim demanded $25,000 in settlement of her claim. When the case went to trial in 1982, the motel offered no defense experts, but the victim's attorney produced a lock expert. In open court, he stated that he had informed the motel management one year prior to the attack, that the motel needed safer locks. Also offered was expert medical testimony that the victim had suffered serious emotional problems as the result of the attack, and a Los Angeles trial jury awarded her $50,000.

In still another example, on a bone chilling day in February 1979, a business woman checked into a motel in Reading, Pennsylvania. Ironically, it was a franchised motel of the same national motel franchisor as above. This guest's motel nightmare is recounted in the following verbatim narrative of the police report:

> Victim stated that she checked into the room around 5 p.m. She left the room and went shopping. She left the room lights on when she left. When she returned, she entered the room, and everything seemed okay. She put a paper bag down near the bathroom, and turned around and was going back to the main area of the room, when she turned around, and she was hit on the back of the head, and knocked down. The subject continued to hit the victim about the face. He attempted to take her coat off, tearing a button off in the process. He then held a hand over the victim's mouth, and removed her shoes, and her panty hose. Victim was struggling to free herself, and subject got off of her, grabbed her pocketbook and fled. Victim stated she did not know what the subject was wearing. All dark clothing, and had a dark ski mask on. Approxi-

mately five feet nine inches tall, build unknown, victim taken to hospital by ambulance.

The assailant was never arrested. The victim filed a lawsuit. Among other things, the suit claimed that the guest room door lock was inadequate, therefore, unsafe. Pre-trial discovery revealed numerous previous crimes on this motel's premises prior to this attack. This lawsuit was concluded in 1982 with a pre-trial settlement of five figures.

Eight months after this violent attack, and just a few guest rooms away, another female guest was sexually assaulted. The victim drove to Reading with two women companions. After checking in, the three guests dined in the motel restaurant. After dinner, the threesome returned to their room, whereupon the victim fell asleep. Her companions decided to visit the motel lounge for a nightcap. Without disturbing their friend, the two women departed the room and went to the motel lounge for a drink.

Shortly after their departure, the lone woman asleep on the bed was startled as she was awakened by a male intruder standing on the side of the bed and touching her. During the next forty-five minutes, the assailant beat, raped and robbed the guest. He made his escape, and was never identified or arrested. Upon the return of her friends, the police were summoned, and the victim was transported to a nearby hospital. After her return home and following partial recovery from the trauma of the vicious attack, this woman filed a lawsuit against the motel. This lawsuit also claimed that the guest room lock was inadequate and therefore, unsafe. During a pre-trial deposition, the police detective who investigated this crime testified that no forced entry on the door jam, lock, or door itself was evident. The officer then answered in the affirmative when asked if the guest lock to the door could be opened, "by a person skilled in burglary, with a credit card or similar device, without leaving signs of forced entry." Evidence in this case clearly demonstrated that the lock was unsafe and could be opened with a credit card. The motel management knew this, as a result of the previous lawsuit. This second case against the motel was concluded with a pre-trial settlement of five figures. It is unknown whether this motel has ever installed safe guest room locks.

Locks, Keys and Doors

The dog-eared newspaper clippings of the past several decades chart the course of notice to the innkeeping industry at large, about the proliferation of violent criminal attacks against the trusting traveling public—"Gunman Shot in Hotel Holdup"— "Robbers Horrify Two Motel Guests"—"Man Guilty in P.G. Motel Murder." Unfortunately, while newspapers across the country were alerting everyone about the problem, most hoteliers chose to ignore it. The history of the innkeeping industry's response to guest security is one of long-lived and monumental indifference. Hoteliers have conspicuously failed to allocate funds for research and development of safe architectural design for their buildings, landscaping, and parking facilities, or even guest room door locks. The traveling public has the right to expect that while inside their guest room, they are secure from criminal attack. If this expectation is invalid, there can be no expectation of guest security anywhere upon the innkeeping premises.

The need for security for persons and property has resulted in the development and improvement of locking devices throughout the ages. Archeological evidence shows that primitive locking devices appeared nearly 4,000 year ago in the Chinese and Hindu cultures. The Egyptian culture improved these devices by developing locks regarded as the prototype of locks used throughout the world today. Theirs required a key to open it, but the lock was vulnerable, because it was designed for use on the exterior of doors. Later, a more highly developed Greek culture designed locks for inside, which could be opened with a key from the exterior. Still later, the Romans fashioned locks from iron and bronze, instead of wood. In so doing, the Romans were able to reduce the size of the lock and keyway, resulting in the reduced size of keys. With further development throughout the centuries, improved locking devices have appeared. The most notable improvements in recent years occurred through the efforts of locksmiths in England and America, in 1778 and 1844, respectively. Rather recently, the electronic locking device has been developed and is today regarded as the state-of-the-art device.

It is not necessary to be a locksmith, or to be conversant in locksmithing nomenclature, to understand the security features necessary to provide a secure lock for use on a hotel or motel's door. There are three basic security features that can be thought of as the ABC principles of a secure guest room lock:

(A) The lock must provide a one-inch dead-bolt, to permit the guest inside the room to shut out all room keys, as well as master keys. (Except the innkeeper emergency master key) It should be automatically disengaged by the guest by turning the inside door knob, in the event that emergency exit from the room becomes necessary.

(B) The lock must provide an automatic spring bolt to assure that whenever the guest room door is in a closed position, the door is automatically locked. Admittance to the guest room can only be accomplished with the use of a key—the outside door knob is always inoperative.

(C) The automatic spring bolt must include a deadlatch, to prevent the spring bolt from being retracted from outside the door, by use of a shim tool, or piece of plastic.

These principles are necessary and must be incorporated in any mechanical or electronic lock for safety and security of guests' rooms. Any guest room lock that does not incorporate these ABC features is not safe and secure. They have been available in locks for many years. Some hoteliers do provide locks for their guests which incorporate these principles; unfortunately, many do not.

During the decade of the seventies, and the ongoing rhetoric by industry leaders about their efforts to protect the traveling public, a court verdict in the State of Florida sent shock waves throughout the innkeeping industry. This was most dramatically felt by the part of the industry operating hotels and motels throughout the Sunshine State. There, a gentleman was viciously attacked and robbed in his guest room. In 1978, a trial court awarded this victim a substantial sum. This court decision was the first in Florida wherein a motel was deemed negligent and liable for damages, in spite of evidence that the motel had used a guest room lock in *common and standard use* throughout the Florida innkeeping industry. The motel was found liable because it did not provide a dead-bolt feature on the lock.

Unless the guest carries and uses an auxiliary locking device while inside the guest room, the dead-bolt is all that can protect him or her, when inside the room, against unauthorized entry by anyone with a room key.

Probably the most commonly found guest room lock in general use throughout the industry is known as a key-in-knob lock. It's name derives from the location of the keyway into which the key is inserted. It is located in the center of the outside door knob. Unfortunately, very few key-in-knob locks installed at the present time offer the security of a secure lock using the ABC principles.

A number of jurisdictions throughout the U.S. have ordinances and building codes that directly effect guest fire safety and, at the same time, guest security. An example of this, is the self-closing devices mandated for hotels and motels in some jurisdictions. Since smoking inside the guest room is a chief cause of innkeeping fires, self-closing devices on guest room doors are desirable from a fire safety perspective. A closed door impedes the spread of fire, acting as a barrier. For instance, several years ago, at the Mayflower Hotel in Washington, D.C., a maid saw smoke coming from beneath a guest room door. Untrained, she opened the door, and was surprised by a room full of smoke. Panicky, she fled the scene, leaving the door open. By the time the D.C. Fire Department appeared, the fire had spread into the corridor. Before this fire was brought under control, almost the entire floor was damaged by smoke. This necessitated putting the damaged floor "off market" for months, while restoration was completed. No fatalities resulted from this fire, but the lost hotel revenue amounted to many thousands of dollars, plus the expense of restoration.

From a security perspective, self-closing door devices are desirable. The purpose of even the best locking device on a guest room door is nullified when the door is not closed. Where installed, self-closing door devices help provide reasonable care by the innkeeper for the guest.

An infrequently recognized guest security breach is the effect that warped or misaligned doors and door frames have on the effectiveness of even the most secure guest room locks. Sadly, this security problem is far more common than generally expected. Warped and misaligned doors and frames can impede the lock from engaging properly. In other instances, the space between the edge of the door and the door frame "strike plate," which receives the spring bolt of the lock, is widened to the point that misalignment occurs. Then the lock can be bypassed with a "shim" tool, or piece of plastic. The convenient plastic "Do Not Disturb" signs hoteliers diligently provide are sometimes used by criminals to slip hotel-motel locks. Even state-of-the-art, electronic locks can be exposed to surreptitious entry. For this reason, it is generally conceded by innkeeping security experts that metal doors and frames are more secure than wood. In turn, solid core wooden doors are superior to others of less weight.

There can be no reasonable level of care for guests if the innkeeper fails to inform them of the operation and functional features of the room lock, as well as other security devices that may be provided inside the room. The innkeeper has a responsibility to encourage their use. Such conduct is prudent and reasonable, considering that the ordinary hotelkeeper does not inform the guest of the type and frequency of crimes on and about the premises. This information about safety and security devices can take the form of written notice inside of the guest room. It should take the form of verbal instruction by employees—front desk personnel, the bellstaff—while rooming the guest. If, during the course of rooming the guest, bellpersons can offer a short discussion to the guest regarding the proper use of the air-conditioning and television, they can easily provide a few moments discussion of the security devices inside the guest room, including the lock. Most guests are appreciative of this concern for their safety, especially women traveling alone. Along these lines, a few hotelkeepers have developed a video for viewing on the guests' television. It describes safety and security measures. The bellperson turns the television channel on to the video when rooming the guest. Unfortunately, this exercise in reasonable care is an uncommon practice in the industry.

When guests are roomed, the management must be certain that all points of entrance to the guest room, such as connecting doors to adjoining guest rooms, patio doors, and even windows, are closed, locked, and secure. Some of the most recently constructed hotels and motels have installed systems that necessitate that the dead-bolt be engaged by the guest once inside the room, for certain objects in the room, such as the television to function. Hotels and motels that have installed such security systems for their guests are to be commended. They are, however, few in number. A recent check on a new property in Florida offering this level of guest security, revealed that the rack rate for guest rooms exceeded $200 per night for single occupancy.

Security negligence can surface in surprising ways. For example, a Dallas, Texas, motel had dutifully installed "peep holes" in all guest room doors. Although they could be observed from the outside, once inside the guest room the "peep hole" was nowhere to be found. It turned out that the motel management had placed the room rate card with fire safety instructions printed on it, directly over the "peep hole," thereby preventing its use by the guest.

In 1982, a young female guest was criminally assaulted inside a Virginia motel room, while her infant child lay asleep in a nearby crib. At issue in the ensuing lawsuit was the guest room door lock, as well as the notice posted on the inside of the door. The innkeeper had placed a notice about fire safety, and at the very bottom of the notice, large print stated that "For your safety, always check to be sure your door is locked. When in your room, secure the auxiliary locking device, too."

The guest door lock used at the motel where this crime occurred did not provide the principles of a secure lock. It had no dead-bolt. The "auxiliary locking device" referred to in the notice to the guest, was merely a security chain, and by definition, a security chain is not a lock. The motel defense counsel dug up two so-called innkeeping security "experts." On behalf of the motel, they testified that the security chain was a lock.

In 1986, an executive of this motel chain was questioned under oath regarding guest security and locks:

Q. To the best of your knowledge, has there ever been any consideration given by you or anybody in management to providing dead-bolt locks on the doors?

A. We have discussed it several times.

Q. Was there a consensus of opinion concerning the implementation of dead-bolt locks?

A. Well, our feeling is that the door chain has worked very well for us. For one thing, it is very visible to the guest. You do not necessarily have that convenience with a dead-bolt—we have a total of about 1200 motel rooms, and we have never had a case of forced entry with a chain being broken or cut, or anything, when a guest was in the room.

Q. Are you aware of any way that a person could get in through a door that was chained without breaking the chain?

A. Not that I am aware of.

The motel executive's testimony is typical of the ordinary industry manager, who is ignorant of the discipline of security and the measures needed to ensure guest safety. Testimony of the two "experts" is indicative of professional industry apologists who have developed a fetish for testifying for negligent innkeepers. The plain truth is that security chains are not locks. Even a dictionary will verify this fact. Security chains can be disengaged with a few thumb tacks and rubber bands, or even a wire coat hanger. This lawsuit was simply another telling fragment of the industry's security problems.

Incidents of forced entry into a guest room by means of damage to the door, frame, or lock is not common, but it does occur. Usually, the availability of room keys to the criminal precludes the need for such measures.

There is an abundance of evidence produced from guest security-related litigation demonstrating that many industry members are too incompetent to keep their establishments' room keys out of the hands of criminals. The Holway lawsuit is one such case in point.

During the latter part of the 1970's, and into the early 1980's, the lock manufacturing industry began marketing locks sophisticated enough to alleviate the guest room key security problem. During this time, locksmithing specialists developed a variety of innovative mechanical and electronic locks for the innkeeping industry's use. By 1980, the Hilton chain had installed an innovative electronic lock on the 38th floor of one of its prestigious New York properties. The lock was still in an experimental stage of application, and once modified, it proved to be successful. Since then, this hotel chain, and others, have installed improved versions of this electronic lock. Other chains have used innovative mechanical locks developed for application within the innkeeping environment. But, such locking devices remain in relatively limited industry use today, compared to the total number of guest rooms offered the public by the industry. The underlying concept behind the development of these improved locks is to provide the newly arrived guest with a fresh key. All previously issued keys will not open the lock. They are also designed to be rekeyed with simplicity and efficiently at the master level. These newer locks incorporate the principles of a secure lock.

The three distinct advantages of these new mechanical and electronic locks are: (1) the locks replace older locks which do not provide the ABC principles; (2) the new locks provide greater protection of guest room property during periods when the room is vacant; and (3) the master level keys can be quickly and effectively changed. These new locks are a positive addition to the mechanics of assuring guest security.

It is the major national and regional hotel-motel chains that most often install the new mechanical and electronic locks on their properties. New properties, and older properties that have undergone major renovations, frequently use these new locking devices, because installation is less expensive during new construction, or during the course of major renovations. The larger chains are in a better financial position than smaller innkeepers to take advantage of the latest safety and security developments.

Not all of the major chains have installed these new locking devices, and fewer still, have installed them on all the guest room doors at all properties. Since most members of the traveling public do not check into $200 and $300 a night hotel rooms, many guests have never seen these state-of-the-art locks, and it probably will be many years before these locks are commonplace throughout the industry.

It should be kept clearly in mind, however, that when a guest is inside his room, and has been provided a door lock with the proper principles, it does not matter whether the lock is a new mechanical or electronic lock, or an older mechanical lock. The guest is as safe and secure as is reasonably possible when the one inch bolt is used, provided of course, that the door and frame are not seriously misaligned. Therefore, the newest mechanical and electronic locks are by no means a panacea, although they are a giant step forward. Interestingly, as recently as 1989, Courtyard by Marriott persisted in placing display ads in national magazines that depict a guest room door complete with an inferior lock.

Since it is reasonable to expect that it will be many years before state-of-the-art locking devices for guest room doors are commonplace throughout the industry, it is necessary to focus attention on the industry's glacial-paced response to the issue of room key security.

Inside a sizeable hotel property, of say eight hundred rooms, there would ordinarily be various levels of keying for guest room locks. Included are an innkeeper's emergency master key, to enable management to open a lock that is dead-bolted from the inside by the guest. Because this most important key can disengage the dead-bolt, it can also engage it when no one is inside the guest room. It is sometimes used for this latter purpose by management, when disputes arise concerning the payment of the guest room bill. In addition, experienced travelers will sometimes ask the hotel or motel to dead-bolt the door when they are not in the guest room, to better protect property inside the room. Few guests, however, are aware of this security measure. This most important key must be kept under very strict security control, because it is capable of opening the guest room door lock, even though the guest is inside and has used the dead-bolt to lock out all other room keys. Small and medium-sized hotels and motels often have this level of keying for guest room door locks.

The next level of keying used in the industry is a master key capable of opening all guest room door locks, as long as the dead-bolt is not engaged. After this, the next level is a floor master. It will open guest room door locks on a specific floor. But not locks that are dead-bolted. The next level of keying is a floor section master which will open a specific number of room locks, usually sixteen, on a specific guest floor. The final level of keying in use is the individual guest room key, and it will not open a lock which is dead-bolted. This level of keying for guest room locks is applicable to the newer mechanical locks, as well as electronic locks. In the latter, the chief difference is the use of a "card key" in place of the conventional metal key.

A large contingent of industry employees such as engineers, housekeeping personnel, and front desk receptionists, by the nature of their work, have access to varying levels of master keys, as well as individual guest room keys. All master keys and individual guest room keys must be strictly controlled by management. The newer electronic locks often provide an audit trail of the date, time, and level of key used to enter the guest room lock. This feature provides an investigative tool regarding theft of property when the guest is out of the room.

No guest room key should have the room number, or hotel address engraved or attached to it. On conventional guest room keys, in lieu of an engraved or attached room number, a numerical code should be engraved or attached that in no way corresponds to the actual room number of the lock the key will open. Upon checking into the property, the guest is furnished the numerically coded guest room key and informed by the front desk receptionist of the room number assigned. The receptionist can also provide the guest with a card with the room number written on it. The guest can trust the room number to memory or refer to the card if necessary. The front desk receptionist maintains a dual security list of room numbers and codes to facilitate the issuance and retrieval of guest room keys. One security list provides the room key codes in numerical sequence, and corresponding room numbers. The other, the room numbers in numerical sequence, and corresponding code key numbers. In this way, by referring to either list, the receptionist can easily match codes with keys, or vice-versa. These security lists are kept at the front desk reception area in a location out of view of the public.

The chief benefit of this security measure is to reduce the number of persons who know what guest room lock a given key will open. It is not perfect. The standard, however, is neither perfection, nor is it zero risk. The standard is reasonable care. The method of using coded keys, is an exercise in reasonable care if the locks themselves are rotated periodically. At least one national hotel chain, Hyatt, has used this security measure of coded guest room keys, and the system has enjoyed widespread public acceptance. It is a security measure that should be in common usage throughout the industry. Unfortunately, it is not.

While the newer, state-of-the-art mechanical and electronic locking devices offer improved guest security, they are not without a degree of risk. For instance, at one hotel property, it was recently discovered that a front desk receptionist was programming all guest room card keys at a master level, then issuing them to newly arriving guests, instead of programming individual room card keys for each new guest. Thus, each newly arriving guest had a card key that would open the locks to all other guest rooms.

Some electronic lock card key systems require guests to remove the card key from the lock after inserting it, before the lock will open. These systems are superior to systems that do not require such an exercise, because it discourages the guest

from inadvertently leaving the card key inside the lock, and closing the door behind. Electronic locks that provide entry systems comprised of push buttons, or which accommodate card
keys that use coded punch-outs resembling a domino are also
available for industry use. However, they are less desirable than
electronic locks that use a magnetic coded card key because
they can be manipulated by knowledgeable criminals. Additionally, electronic locks that feature a master emergency mechanical key are less desirable than electronic locks that require the
use of a magnetically coded master emergency card key.

Innkeeping guest room locks that do not incorporate the
features of the ABC principles are a mechanical failure. And
installing them in hotels and motels represents a human failure.
Too frequently, just a few feet from the chocolates on the
pillows, is a guest room door with an unsafe lock, and too
many strangers with the keys to open it. This is due to conduct
by hotelkeepers who have created an upside-down world of
innkeeping, wherein necessities are luxuries, and luxuries are
necessities.

Four

Shroud of Secrecy—Shattered

They put their trust in the advertising of a well-known chain, but JoAnn and Jack Bradford were betrayed. In the early morning hours of a hot July day, they innocently opened the door to their motel room and were suddenly trapped in a very dark drama.

JoAnn and Jack had been born and reared in Kentucky, then got married, and moved to the Midwest. With their two children, Beth, age 19 and Shaun, age 17, the Bradfords, in many ways, epitomized an average American family.

The Bradford family embarked upon a long, anticipated vacation. They drove their Pontiac to Little Rock, Arkansas, where they stayed overnight in a motel, before proceeding to Dallas to visit JoAnn's brother. The family checked into a nationally advertised budget motel, located on Hawn Freeway. It was still daylight when they parked directly in front of their room and carted their luggage inside. Beth and her father visited the swimming pool, as JoAnn remained in the guest room, took a bath, and prepared for bed. Shaun had remained at the home of JoAnn's brother and his wife. JoAnn's niece, also a teenager, decided to join the Bradfords at the motel, and to stay over with them. About midnight, all were asleep inside their room.

JoAnn was a light sleeper, so she was the first to be awakened by the knocking on an adjacent guest room door. Then she heard a loud knock on her door, and asked her husband to see what was going on. Jack dutifully stumbled out of bed. Somewhere between being asleep and awake, Jack Bradford opened the door to see who had rudely awakened him, and what they wanted.

Assumably, guests of hotels or motels are preoccupied with the purpose of their travel, business or pleasure. In any case, the last thing on their minds is that they might be selected by a predator to become the victim of a violent crime. The Bradford family knew nothing of the nature and frequency of violent crime at this motel. If guests realized that they might become victims, or the thought even crossed their minds, they certainly wouldn't open their guest room door indiscriminately. But, largely because of the industry's advertising, suggesting safe conditions, guests have come to regard themselves as safe within the innkeeping environment.

JoAnn heard someone at the door ask her husband for "John Foley." She started to lay her head back down on the pillow. The next thing she heard was the door's being forced open and saw her husband knocked to the floor. One intruder held a gun to her husband's head as another assailant jumped on the bed, putting a large knife to JoAnn's throat.

The trespasser with the gun threatened to blow Jack's head off. All the occupants of this room were robbed of their money and Jack was beaten in front of the three women. The intruders then forced all four guests into the bathroom. Systematically, each of the three women were removed, one by one, taken into the sleeping area of the small room, and criminally assaulted. The sordid details of the events which occurred within the four walls of the small guest room, are unworthy of being described here, but they are contained in the transcripts of the sworn testimony of the lawsuit that resulted.

After the attack, the two assailants departed the motel premises, and were never identified, arrested or prosecuted for their despicable acts.

After collecting their wits and getting dressed, the four distraught guests left the crime scene, and walked directly to the motel office. They rang the night buzzer, beat upon the motel office windows and shouted for several minutes, but nobody came to help. Realizing that there would be no aid from the motel, the guests got into their car and drove down Hawn Freeway. They found an all-night service station and a sympathetic attendant summoned help for them. The police arrived and escorted the guests back to the motel, and then to the same hospital where President Kennedy had died from an assassin's bullet. That night, the family stayed with relatives and the following day, they departed Dallas and drove directly, non-stop back to their home.

The lawsuit which Jack and JoAnn filed against the motel many months later provided yet another view of negligent guest security practices. Lawsuits related to guest security are usually filed months after the guest is victimized, and it is sometimes several years before a trial date for such a civil case is set on a court calendar. During the time between the crime committed against the Bradford family, and the trial date for their lawsuit against the motel, evidence was revealed that almost defies imagination.

Shortly before the visit of the Bradford family to the motel, a new manager and his wife assumed responsibility for operating the property. The manager arrived fresh after a seven-day training period provided by the motel chain. The motel chain prides itself on hiring husband and wife management teams for their properties. In turn, they provide their managers and spouses spartan living quarters, located upon the motel premises, and a modest salary to match.

This particular motel had experienced several armed robberies prior to the assault of the Bradford family, including one attack just a few weeks before the arrival of the new manager. The new one-inch thick bullet resistant glass that protected the front office area, where the cashier took the guest's money, attested to that fact. The motel had also installed a dead-bolt lock on the door to the front desk office to protect the manager. At 11:00 p.m. sharp, the front office closed. In order for travelers to obtain service between 11:00 p.m. and 7:00 a.m., members of the public were informed via a large sign to use a buzzer to summon assistance. This buzzer had been installed to alert the manager inside his living quarters. During trial preparation, it was never established whether the buzzer was working the night of the Bradford's ordeal, or whether the manager simply chose to ignore the buzzer. In either case, the result was the same.

Like most hotelkeepers, this budget motel chain was keenly aware of aesthetics. Although it was expensive to install and maintain, an outdoor swimming pool was provided for guests to use during hot Texas summer days. But under the pretext of economy, this motel operation offered nothing in terms of guest security. It did not even provide telephones inside the rooms.

The following are excerpts from the transcript of the sworn testimony of the senior vice president of this national motel corporation:

Q. Are part of your duties and responsibilities to help formulate policies regarding security features in the units, or security procedures that should be used by the units?

A. Help, yes.

Q. Who else helps formulate those policies?

A. The input from the quarterly meetings of problems, comes back to the office.

Q. This input is from regional vice-presidents?

A. Yes, sir.

Q. Okay. Now, also, do some of the people on the board, or the officers in the company, besides you, have something to do with formulating security policies?

A. Yes sir.

Q. Is there any part of the office that is bulletproof?

A. There is the night window, which the manager works out of after the office is closed, whatever time operations determines the time to close the office. And then they work out of the night window.

Q. Okay. Now is that night window bulletproof?

A. Yes sir, bullet resistant.

Q. Why is it bullet resistant?

A. Just for a little protection for the man at night.

Q. Can you think of any other features of the office that might be considered to be security features?

A. There is a steel panel under the window to the floor.

Q. And what is that for?

A. So the manager can stand by the window and still not be shot through the wall under it.

Q. Okay. What are the security features that are put into the individual rooms in the standard motel unit?

A. There are no special security features.

Q. Do you know of any of your units that do have peepholes, or observation ports, in the door?

A. Not that I'm aware of.

Q. Okay. One of the functions of the peephole is so you can see who is out there in front of your door. Wouldn't that be fair to say?

A. If you're tall enough to get your eye to it, yes.

Q. Well don't they also have peepholes that they put in some places for wheelchair people?

A. They may. I'm not aware of it.

Q. Would you agree with me that a peephole would be a good security feature to have in a motel room?

A. Not as a flat statement, I wouldn't agree with you.

Q. Do you know of any of your motel units that have a chain on the door?

A. Not of my own knowledge.

Q. Do you know why they don't have telephones in the motel rooms now?

A. Mainly because we are a budget or economy motel.

Q. Would you agree that having a telephone in an individual room would be a good security feature for a motel?

A. Yes.

Q. Do you know if your motel units normally have a plaque or something in the room that gives security information to the customers?

A. Not that I know of.

Q. Do you know whether the motel managers are instructed to have regular security meetings with their staff to discuss security problems?

A. I don't know what the procedures are.

Q. Do you know whether any insurance carrier has ever asked your motel company to change any safety or security features, or add new safety or security features to the rooms?

A. Not that I'm aware of.

Q. Well, do you have the authority to make changes in safety procedures or features yourself?
A. Personally do it, no.
Q. How would you go about doing it, if you wanted to, or try to get it done?
A. It should be brought up when we have a standards committee meeting.
Q. Well at these standard committee meetings, have you ever discussed adding chain locks to the rooms?
A. Not that I recall.
Q. Have you ever discussed adding peepholes to the rooms?
A. Not that I recall.
Q. Have you ever discussed adding telephones to the rooms?
A. Not that I recall.

Such testimony might be expected from a motel executive in a Third World country, but it is nothing less than scandalous in America. Similar negligent conditions continue today on a nationwide scope in hotels and motels.

The Bradford family was most fortunate to have engaged the services of a young attorney who worked in the offices of one of the most prominent personal injury trial attorneys in the Southwest United States. The lawsuit was set for trial in March, 1983. This trial date was postponed, and in July of 1983, the motel chain settled the lawsuit with Jack and JoAnn Bradford in the amount of $450,000. Of course, hotelkeepers do not pay thousands of dollars to guests who are the victims of violent hotel-motel crimes, unless the guest has a case. This national motel chain has been sued on a number of occasions for cases involving rapes, robberies, assaults and murders on their properties.

Litigation and Settlements

All victims don't sue; unfortunately, excellent attorneys are not available to every guest who is the victim of negligent conduct by hoteliers. There is little doubt that the reputation, skills, and personal ability of an attorney who represents an injured guest often marks the distinction between victory or defeat in a courtroom trial and can also have a dynamic influence upon out-of-court settlement negotiations. In some instances, the reputation and credentials of expert witnesses can also have a dynamic influence on the outcome of a lawsuit.

With the rising costs associated with going to trial, it has become increasingly necessary for most attorneys to examine a case very carefully. If potential recovery is not well within six figures, many trial attorneys will not accept the case. Wrongful death cases, like the one filed by the parents of Dr. Emerson, or personal injury cases such as the Butler case, which result in serious physical or mental impairment and have "jury appeal," often merit awards in the hundreds of thousands of dollars.

Most personal injury attorneys represent the victim on a contingency basis. If the attorney wins the case for the client, he or she is ordinarily paid approximately one-third of the award, or settlement, plus expenses. If they lose, they are usually paid nothing. It is a matter of taking a risk. After a lawsuit is filed and progresses, expenses add up. Investigators, expert witnesses, and shorthand reporters have to be paid.

On occasion, the plaintiff's attorney spends thousands of dollars as "front money" in a case to pay for the expenses incurred in pursuing a lawsuit. The client in such circumstances has no resources to pay. An attorney who does this is convinced that the case has merit and is winnable.

The expenses associated with an important case can be substantial. In the Emerson case in Norfolk, the identity of Mr. Owens, the guest who reported the trespassers, was not voluntarily revealed by the defendant motel. Once identified, he had to be located by an investigator and persuaded to give trial testimony. This was done through the efforts of a competent investigator who was retained full-time by the law firm that represented the decedent's parents. Then, qualified innkeeping security experts needed to be located. They had to be consulted regarding various security aspects of the case. Additionally, the experts had to be flown to Norfolk for trial testimony. Winning can be expensive, even when you have a good case.

Although industry policies and practices in regard to guest security bespeak negligence, much of it is hidden. Discovering this hidden negligence is a difficult task. There is no greater service to the public by the legal profession, than the representation of countless guests who have become injured victims of violent crime as the result of the negligent security policies and practices. The lawsuit is the nemesis of the negligent hotelkeeper.

The adversarial system of guest security-related litigation ordinarily sets into motion the rivalry of two markedly unequal opponents—the individual of limited resources and innkeeping businesses of seemingly unlimited resources. Within the corporate executive suites sit the decision makers when it comes to guest security policies and practices. There is little, if any, accountability of the conduct of corporate executives. The individual victim, with limited resources and seeking redress through the judicial system has only one opportunity. By contrast, hotel and motel chains lose countless guest security-related lawsuits with virtually no adverse effect. The losses do not even make the pie charts in the annual report. Major innkeeping corporations annually pay out millions of dollars in nationwide claims, court awards and settlements, and then each year proceed to raise room rates, go on with business as usual, and continue prospering. Smaller, independent hotelkeepers are less insulated against penalties than the large corporations, but to a certain extent, they too, enjoy a financial edge over the victim bringing suit.

It should be kept firmly in mind that major corporations conducting the business of innkeeping can, and in fact usually do, retain the best legal counsel available to defend themselves from the standard of penalties for any negligence. No matter how unpopular or how untenable the hotelier's position may be in adjudicated guest security matters, they are usually defended by the most elite law firms in the nation. Defense attorneys who represent these prosperous innkeepers don't do business on a contingency basis and are ordinarily paid by the hour for their services. The longer the meter runs, the wealthier their law firms become. It is little wonder so many cases the industry loses in trial courts are brought before the appellate court system.

It is sheer fiction to think that law firms defend negligent innkeepers because of an unwavering fidelity to the adversary system. Without the enormous fees paid to them by negligent hotelkeepers, and the insurance companies that indemnify them, most of these law firms would not touch the average guest security-related lawsuit.

However, it should not be inferred that members of the inn-keeping industry should be deprived of their right to the best legal counsel they can afford to defend proper conduct, and protect assets and reputation. Defense attorneys who defend such hotelkeepers render a necessary service to the industry, as well as society as a whole.

Members of the public are certainly known to initiate spurious, even frivolous claims against hotelkeepers. Regretfully, these litigants can usually find personal injury trial attorneys to champion their cause. Cupidity afflicts many. It is never in the interests of anyone that a counterfeit claim or lawsuit without merit—regarded as a nuisance suit—enjoy any measure of success, regardless in what garment of respectability it may be dressed.

Since our society has become increasingly litigious, greater numbers of victims of hotel-motel crimes have sought to participate in the litigation process. As a result, a number of special interest groups have reacted by supporting the enactment of legislation that would cap the amount a trial jury can award a victim. Insurance companies, as well as various segments of the business community, have vociferously supported such efforts to set a limit to jury awards—known as tort reforms. They support this move because it would offer smaller awards to the victim in lawsuits. Thus far, tort reform measures, which would certainly affect litigation involving the innkeeping industry, have realized limited success.

Lawsuits filed against members of the industry alleging a breach of duty to provide reasonable care are seldom brought to the trial stage. The vast majority of guest security lawsuits are settled out of the courtroom, long before any trial date. They are often settled for substantial amounts.

Thus, actual court room dramas, such as those that unfolded in the Emerson or Butler lawsuits, are really only the small, visible tip of the litigation iceberg. Out-of-court settlements, such as the Bradford case, represent the more extensive, hidden portion of guest security cases that remain generally unknown, and unrecognized.

It is this hidden side of innkeeping that industry trade associations, and industry defense legal teams, ardently try to hide from the public's scrutiny, with good reason. It is the underside of the industry that exposes negligent policies and practices.

Litigation involving guest security is a fascinating part of American jurisprudence, and in many respects it is a game of skill as well as chance. To be sure, powerful forces are at play. The game has rules, players, winners and losers.

Nationwide, security-related lawsuits against hotelkeepers serve as a repository of innkeeping industry mismanagement, mistreatment, and misconduct. If one tried to determine the numbers of security-related lawsuits filed against a particular hotel or motel chain, it would be necessary to visit the civil records division of federal and state court systems in every jurisdiction in which the chain operates hotels or motels. Locating these lawsuits would be a complex and tedious process impeded by an arcane, and often archaic judicial filing system, rendering such an effort virtually impossible. But worse, a sizeable number of these lawsuits against hotelkeepers will not show how the case was finally resolved, because secret settlement agreements preclude such disclosure—to protect the reputation of the negligent hotelkeeper.

Understanding the litigation process requires familiarity with some basic information in order to acquaint oneself with just how negligent hotelkeepers, and the attorneys defending them, play the game—and try to hide the blame. In reality, the civil judiciary system lends itself to litigants, and their attorneys, more interested in winning cases than seeking justice.

The lawsuit over guest security begins with the filing of a complaint before a court having jurisdiction over the subject matter to be litigated. The party who begins the case is the plaintiff; the party sued, the defendant. There can be more than one plaintiff and more than one defendant named in the complaint. Defendants can be business entities, such as the franchisee and franchisor corporation, or individuals, such as managers, directors of security, or other named and unnamed employees of the innkeeper.

The complaint will allege that the defendant violated his duty to the plaintiff to provide reasonable care against foreseeable harm from the misconduct of a third party, who is the criminal that attacked the guest. The alleged violations of duty will be specified in the complaint, and where germane, the complaint will address such guest security concerns as key control, guest room door locks, lighting of the premises, employee training and staffing, as well as security patrols of the premises. The plaintiff will allege in the complaint that one or more of the breaches of duty specified was what is termed a proximate cause, of injury to the plaintiff. Proximate cause is legal cause, and does not need to be *the* cause, or the *only* cause, but it must be a *significant, and a predominant cause* of injury to the plaintiff. Proximate cause links evidence of a breach of duty to actual injury. Evidence of a breach of duty that can be demonstrated to have been a foreseeable proximate cause of injury to the plaintiff, is sufficient in most cases for the court to find the hotelkeeper negligent. In considering breaches of duty, and their foreseeable relationship to proximate causes, the courts have considered such diverse matters as geographic location, building and landscaping design, occupancy rates, type of clientele and the type and frequency of crime on the premises, as well as crimes in the immediate and surrounding area.

The legal issue of foreseeability is one that deserves particular attention, because negligent hotelkeepers often choose this issue as the primary justification for their failure to provide adequate protection against crime. Indeed, transcripts of sworn testimony of those who earn their living by serving as "expert witnesses" for hotelkeepers and in turn the defense attorneys, reveal a degree of preoccupation with the elusive issue of fore-seeability.

This issue of foreseeability is elusive because of the absence of legislation to establish in law any standards for the performance of guest security. And, of course, the initial victim of any crime has difficulty seeking justice. In addition, various courts within the judicial system have clouded the legal concept of foreseeability by applying it to the duty to provide reasonable care, as well as proximate cause. Within the context of foreseeability, and for the purposes of informed comparison, the dual public safety issues of guest security and guest fire safety are similar.

Hotel-motel fires are regarded as foreseeable events. Statutes and ordinances have been promulgated, which require hotels and motels to provide minimal protection in the form of portable fire extinguishers, and designated fire exits. These forms of public protection must be provided to protect the guest, even if the premises has never had a fire. Yet, except for arson fires, all fires of known origin are classified as accidents. And, an accident is defined as an unplanned event.

By contrast, violent crimes are regarded as unforeseeable events. But crimes are not accidents; they are planned. Like the crime of arson, crimes result from planned, willful misconduct. Therefore, it is illogical to reason that fires, which are accidents and unplanned, are foreseeable, while crime, not an accident and planned, is somehow *unforeseeable*. This dichotomy of foreseeability is attributable, in large measure, to the failure of security practitioners to clearly explain the principles of the discipline of security.

Almost every kind of crime that has ever been conjured from the dark recesses of the human mind has, at one time or another, been committed within the environment of hotels or motels. In the climate of epidemic violent crime that now plagues our society, it seems ludicrous to claim that violent crime in hotels or motels is somehow unforeseeable.

In filing a complaint at law, the plaintiff seeks compensatory damages, and sometimes asks for punitive damages. Compensatory damages represent compensation for actual losses such as medical expenses, loss of income, or pain and mental suffering which may accrue from the injury sustained by the victim. In seeking punitive damages, however, the plaintiff seeks to have the court punish the negligent innkeeper. Punitive damages are provided under civil law as prison terms and fines are under criminal cases. The amount of punitive damages sought by the plaintiff against a hotel or motel defendant will almost always far exceed the amount sought for compensatory damages. In awarding punitive damages, the court intends to deter any future undesirable conduct by the hotelkeeper, as well as discourage similar conduct by other members of the industry. Considering the overall picture of the industry's security problems, it would seem that too few plaintiffs' attorneys seek punitive damages for their clients.

The thought of being on the losing end of a punitive damage award is enough to start the heart of even the most unresponsive, negligent hotelkeeper, since many innkeepers operate hotels and motels without indemnification against punitive charges. One reason for this is that, at present, several states in the nation prohibit indemnification against punitive damages. Legislative prohibition currently exists in New York, Ohio, Maine, North Dakota, Kansas, Minnesota, Colorado, and California. The legislators in these states wisely reasoned that a negligent business entity, innkeeping establishments included, should not be able to insure itself against punishment. Where available, insurance coverage for punitive damages is still difficult to acquire. Often, the premium is so costly that few hoteliers can afford it. Obviously, the financial implications for smaller hoteliers, who are assessed punitive damages without insurance protection, can be frightening. It should be noted that at present, ten states limit the amount of punitive damage awards and five states prohibit them entirely.

In a recent security-related lawsuit against a well-known casino hotel, a guest was violently assaulted in a parking ramp elevator. She sued the casino hotel, and was awarded $45,000 in compensatory damages, however the woman was awarded $1 million in punitive damages. Many casino hotels, in Reno, Las Vegas and Atlantic City, are known to provide extensive security to protect revenue and assets. But on the other hand, they often maintain a questionable level of guest security.

In this case, the court concluded that the casino hotel earned ample profits to install closed circuit television cameras in guest areas. In fact, the hotel had placed signs in the ramp area indicating such security equipment was in use, when it was non-existent. The trial court found this hotelkeeper's conduct "inept security" and assessed the punitive damages on behalf of the plaintiff.

There is little doubt that legislation to eliminate or reduce punitive damages would retard an innkeeper's incentive to improve conditions bearing upon the public's safety. On the other hand, it is difficult to imagine the necessity of excessive punitive damage awards that result in bankruptcy or deter insurance companies from doing business in a given state. It is obvious that great wisdom must be brought to bear upon the issue of tort reform legislation, in order to bring balance to the legitimate interests of all the parties concerned.

Another legal concept upon which an injured guest may seek compensation from an innkeeper is warranties. There are two types of warranties. First, express warranty is the oral or written representation made by a seller to a buyer. And second, implied warranty is the inherent representation made by the seller to the buyer. The innkeeper, or seller, is a merchant of lodging quarters and warrants that the lodging offered to the public is safe, and this is implied in the selling of lodging to the guest, who is the buyer.

When the parties to an innkeeping lawsuit reside in different states, as is often the circumstance, the lawsuit usually is brought before a court within the Civil Division of the Federal Court System. Some attorneys prefer to file their client's case before the Federal Judiciary, because they regard the procedures and rules of the federal system to be superior, in some ways, to those of some state court systems. The federal court system is comprised of ninety-four district courts and one court of appeals, for each of thirteen judicial circuits, as well as the Supreme Court of the U.S. The federal system of courts is divided into two general classes—criminal and civil.

Each state court system functions independently from other state jurisdictions, therefore, a decision by the highest state court in Virginia is not binding upon a court in another state, although it may be binding upon lower courts within Virginia. One federal Circuit Court of Appeals may reach a decision concerning a similar legal matter that differs from that of another federal Circuit Court of Appeals. Unless the U.S. Supreme Court renders a decision in the matter, the differing decisions of two different appeals courts are left standing in their respective jurisdictions.

A number of legal matters command the attention of a plaintiff attorney, however he cannot win a lawsuit that fails to prove: (1) the innkeeper had a legal duty to provide reasonable care to protect the plaintiff from dangerous acts or conditions foreseeable; (2) that the defendant innkeeper failed to do so; (3) that this failure was in fact the significant and predominant cause of injury to the guest; (4) that the guest sustained actual injury and harm.

Until recently, a guest who had been the victim of a violent criminal act was unable to recover from a negligent hotelier, if the latter could demonstrate to the court that the guest had been even partially responsible for the injury incurred. This is contributory negligence, and has served the interests of the industry for years. The concept of contributory negligence has had a number of detractors within both the legal and academic communities over the years. Fortunately, their voices have been heard, and at present thirty eight states have replaced the contributory negligence standard with a saner idea; comparative negligence. Comparative negligence holds both defendant and plaintiff at fault, according to degree of negligence. This concept of comparative negligence permits a plaintiff to recover damages, as long as the fault of the plaintiff is not 50% or more.

During the period between the date the complaint is filed and the trial date set by the court, the victim's lawyers open innkeeping closets and expose skeletons. This is the pre-trial discovery. Pre-trial discovery is a two-way street. The plaintiff is also subject to investigation by defense counsel. But the very nature of the litigation lends itself to a greater degree of inquiry by the plaintiff's counsel.

As the pre-trial discovery phase progresses, a plaintiff's attorney will sometimes obtain a court order, to inspect the innkeeping premises, as was done in the case of Connie Francis. Employees are often interviewed, especially former employees, because with the industry's high attrition rate, few current employees would have the information sought during the discovery process. Business records are often subpoenaed. Written questions, called interrogatories, are submitted to both defendant, and plaintiff, requiring answers given under oath. The interrogatories usually will seek documents and records related to staffing schedules, training manuals, guest room door locks, lighting conditions, or key control policies.

Another procedure conducted in preparation for trial is the taking of depositions. Depositions are oral questions and answers that are recorded by a shorthand reporter. The answers are given under oath. The plaintiff's attorney will depose the defendants, as well as various employees of the defendant innkeeper. Plaintiffs are also deposed. During the course of a deposition, it is not surprising to find a witness for the defendant hotel or motel purposely try to "stonewall" or to mislead the attorney, such as the testimony of the chief engineer for the hotel in the Holway case. When questioned about the innkeeper's emergency master key, this engineer responded that the "E" engraved into the key identified it as an engineer key— when in fact, the "E" identifies it as the innkeeper's emergency master key. It will open the guest room door when it is deadbolted from the inside. This testimony under oath by the chief engineer was deceptive. According to written corporate security policies, this engineer and his assistant should not have been permanently issued this most important of hotel keys. They should never have been allowed to carry the keys around on their person throughout the day.

During pre-trial discovery, hotelkeepers commonly hide evidence of alleged negligent conduct through the machinations of their attorneys, by means of protective court orders. A protective court order is part of court secrecy procedures. Often they are used by negligent hotelkeepers to prevent disclosure of damning evidence. Although obtaining them is not uncommon, it is not done in every case, and such an effort is not always successful.

On March 20, 1985, an elderly woman was robbed and brutally assaulted in the parking lot of a hotel in Missouri operating as a Hilton. The woman, in her late seventies, sustained serious injuries, including a fractured hip and wrist. A sizeable lawsuit of a quarter of a million dollars for compensatory damages was filed. Previous assaults and robberies had occurred on and near the hotel premises prior to this assault and logically, were the subject of inquiry and investigation by plaintiff's counsel. In the natural course of events, counsel did this to gather evidence of foreseeability on the part of the hotelkeeper. Counsel sought the sworn testimony by two individuals, and further, to obtain hotel documentation regarding "criminal acts occurring at the hotel, before plaintiff's robbery." But, the hotel sought relief through court secrecy procedures. It petitioned the court to block the depositions and grant the hotel a "protective order" preventing disclosure of any of the alleged incriminating documentation sought by the plaintiff. Although the public seldom knows it, these legal tactics on the part of the innkeeping industry occur frequently. They are a curious display of conduct by an industry which adamantly denies the existence of guest security problems, and professes to serve the public interests so loyally.

In the case in Missouri, a protective order was granted by the Highest Authority—the plaintiff passed from this life into the next from natural causes—and the lawsuit was withdrawn.

Court secrecy procedures have come under increasing criticism from consumer advocacy groups, as well as plaintiff attorneys. Legislation aimed at curbing court secrecy has been brought before state lawmakers and Congress. A 1990 *Washington Post* article reported that the Texas Supreme Court had restricted court secrecy rules for Texas judges. The newspaper quoted the president of the Association of Trial Lawyers of America, Russ Herman, as saying the rule change "is a big win for America's victims and consumers."

As the pre-trial discovery period progresses, the deposition of experts retained by opposing counsel is sought. Experts from the medical profession will testify with respect to injuries, especially psychological damage, sustained by the plaintiff. Physicians who treated the plaintiff may be called upon to testify. The testimony of an expert witness, either in deposition or during the trial, differs from that of other witnesses, in that experts may express their *opinions*, with respect to their areas of expertise concerning the issues before the court. In fact, it is their opinions that are sought.

Unfortunately, the rules governing the qualifications of experts within both federal and state court systems leaves much to be desired. Virtually anyone with knowledge on a particular subject which exceeds the ordinary lay person's, can testify as an expert. Then the jury determines the credibility of this person's testimony.

An innkeeping security expert should have knowledge exceeding that of an ordinary innkeeping security practitioner. Considering the abysmal lack of training in this industry at all levels of security personnel, common sense dictates that a substantial degree of attention should be given to the issue of an expert's "hands on" experience. In reality, an innkeeping security expert is a liability expert. With increasing frequency, short tenured directors of security, as well as members of the academic community, offer incredulous testimony as defense "experts" in guest security-related litigation. Such testimony bears little distinction from the testimony of the industry's "excuse managers" and industry apologists. It appears that when juries hear such testimony, they are unimpressed. After all, the industry loses far more lawsuits than it wins.

The period between the filing of the lawsuit and the cut-off date for discovery, sometimes embracing several years, nearly always unmasks an innkeeping guest security charade. It reveals a clearly discernible pattern of negligent conduct. It is this negligence that is the correlate cause of adjudicated guest security matters.

As evidence of neglect adds up, it refutes the claim of innocence by the defendant hotelkeeper. It undermines any viable defense effort. It sharply reduces the defendant's options. The plaintiff's attorney soon realizes that the fruits of evidence harvested during discovery have enhanced the opportunity for courtroom victory. By contrast, the defendant's attorney has harvested little. Time itself is now the plaintiff's friend—the defendant's enemy. The longer the case runs, the more it costs the defendant.

During this period of unfavorable evidence against the defendant, serious negotiations begin, and deals are made. All kinds of deals. Virtually any agreement that is legal and meets with the approval of their clients, can be struck by the opposing attorneys. For instance, in one guest security-related lawsuit, the plaintiff agreed to drop a defendant from the case, in exchange for the defendant's agreeing to forego appealing a plaintiff verdict, as long as it was not in excess of a mutually acceptable figure. In this case, the plaintiff verdict was an award in the amount of the cap agreed upon. Consequently, there were no post-verdict motions of appeal. The plaintiff's award was close to $500,000.

By the time serious pre-trial negotiations take place, both sides want to avoid the courtroom for a variety of reasons. There is an understandable desire by the plaintiff to avoid reliving their experience in court. Next, the judge assigned to the case, after reviewing the evidence, and consulting counsel, may conclude that the court's time should not be spent on trial. The judge may attempt to persuade the attorneys to settle out-of-court. Obviously, it is not in the best interests of a negligent hotelkeeper to go to trial.

The winning card during settlement negotiation is secrecy. The extent of the negligence by the hotelkeeper, ability to pay, the extent of the plaintiff's damages, and the extent of the public's perception of the reputation of the defendant all bear directly upon how much the plaintiff will be rewarded and the terms of the settlement agreement.

By agreeing beforehand to accept a specified sum of money, the plaintiff will be asked by the defendant to avoid discussing the case, or the terms and amount of the settlement. Once these matters are agreed upon by both sides, the court will confer its blessings upon the settlement and place a "gag order" on the parties, to the relief of the negligent hotelkeeper. The plaintiff's benefit is receiving a substantial sum of money in compensation for experiencing a hotel-motel nightmare, and the avoidance of reliving that nightmare in a trial.

The benefits accrued to the defendant hotelkeeper is to have avoided: media publicity; possible assessment of large punitive damages; the finding of guilt by a jury; courtroom scrutiny of negligent guest security policies and practices; and the cold pointing public finger of condemnation.

For the hotelkeeper involved in a guest security-related lawsuit, the issue is not winning or losing, but hiding the blame.

Occasionally, hotelkeepers and their insurers will settle a security-related lawsuit even though the plaintiff refuses to agree not to disclose information about the case. This is what happened in the lawsuit that resulted from the rape of a guest at a Motel 6 in Fort Worth in September, 1988. The case was featured in a July 18, 1991, *Wall Street Journal* article that focused on the crime problems of the Holiday Inn, Days Inn and Motel 6 innkeeping chains.

The woman, traveling alone and on business, checked into the motel on a Sunday. She inquired whether the motel provided security and was told by the manager that the motel did. Security officers were provided, but only on Friday and Saturday. An ex-convict and a friend were loitering in the parking area on Monday evening when they observed the guest enter her room. The guest's assailants were subsequently arrested and the ex-convict pled quilty to rape. He later testified for the plaintiff in the lawsuit. Although the plaintiff would not agree to a pre-trial settlement that included a confidentiality clause, Motel 6 and its insurers settled this lawsuit in June, 1991, for $10 million.

Nevertheless, the usual results of the efforts of defense attorneys to settle these cases, insulates and protects the very people most responsible for the industry's negligence.

Administrative Remedy

The most effective tactic for hotelkeepers to hide the effects of crime is the practice of administrative remedy. Its use has the effect of thwarting any claim of negligence against the hotel.

For example, during a seasonal period of low occupancy, just before Christmas, a union official checked into a large, prestigious hotel in Washington, D.C. The guest was booked for several days. He was getting dressed on the morning of the second day when he responded to a loud knock on his door. Upon opening the door, this union official was immediately forced back by two assailants, one of whom was armed with a gun. The guest was pistol-whipped, robbed, and tied up before the robbers departed. From beginning to end, the violent scenario lasted perhaps ten to fifteen minutes. After freeing himself, the guest dialed the hotel operator, and hotel security officers responded. The police were summoned, but an investigation never resulted in an arrest.

At the time that this attack occurred, the department of hotel security was seriously understaffed, a fact well known to the hotel general manager. This manager had refused requests to hire security officers, citing the "slow season." Many, but not all, hotels and motels experience reduced occupancy during the month of December. Of course, one of the periods of greater risk of robbery for the guest exists when fewer staff are present and occupancy is low because robbery is a crime of victim isolation. The general manager was informed of this vulnerability by the director of security on several occasions prior to the robbery of the union official. But, true to an established pattern, he chose to ignore the condition and gamble with the public's safety.

On the first day after the crime, the director of security interviewed the victim at least twice. During these interviews, the guest expressed concern about $1,700 cash he had reported to the police as stolen from him during the robbery. The guest told the security director, "I came here with $1,700 and I want to leave with $1,700." At one point during an interview, the guest placed a call to attorneys at the union headquarters concerning his situation.

The highlights of these interviews were conveyed to the general manager, who called the hotel chain's corporate counsel. The general manager then authorized the hotel comptroller to draw a check in the amount of $1,700.00. When this check was furnished to the guest, he was requested to sign a statement absolving the hotel of any negligence concerning the robbery. It contained a clause acknowledging that the statement was signed without duress. Since he was most eager to be reimbursed for the money he had lost, the guest signed without hesitation. About six months later, during the summer months, the director of security encountered the same union official in the hotel lobby. The guest was in Washington on another business trip and surprisingly had checked into the same hotel. The two men spoke briefly, but their conversation was sufficiently long for the guest to recount the ordeal of the heart attack he suffered a month after his last visit to the hotel, where he had suffered a beating and robbery.

It would be considered speculative to conclude that the heart attack resulted from the hotel robbery and attack. Yet, the union official's experience recalls the earlier mentioned attack on Melissa Butler and her husband in Concord, N.C. In that 1988 case, the Appeals Court noted that medical evidence linked the crime at the motel to the heart attack suffered by Mrs. Butler fourteen months later, and upheld the trial court's award. But, for the union official, there would be no trial because of the hotel's use of an administrative remedy.

Five

The Relative Risks

I t was all but impossible to observe the dignified man and his condition, and fail to be touched with compassion. It was a sobering scene. There the man stood—slightly bent and grey. With determination, he took a measured step with his right foot, then dragged his left foot forward, and planted it. His left arm hung immobile. His devoted wife walked very slowly beside him. Her countenance reflected admiration for the labored efforts of her husband. In this manner, they made their way from the quiet corridor into the austere atmosphere of the U.S. District courtroom in Alexandria, Virginia. On this clear, crisp, sunny September morning in 1982, Sam Vogel had traveled to the imposing old Alexandria federal court building to seek justice.

Nearly a year before, Mr. Vogel had been enjoying far better health. He was in his fifties and a traveling salesman working out of North Carolina. He had checked into a pleasant appearing, sixty-room budget motel in Woodbridge, Virginia, roughly 30 miles south of Washington, D.C. The motel was operated as a franchised property of EconoLodge, headquartered in the Southeast.

Within the hour or so after Sam Vogel had checked in, he went out to the parking lot to get some supplies from his car. It was about 6:00 p.m. He paid scant attention to the three youths loitering near their automobile parked next to his. After gathering his supplies, Mr. Vogel walked the hundred feet or so across the parking lot, back toward his ground-floor guest room. Reaching his room, he inserted his key into the center of the doorknob and opened the door.

Suddenly without warning, Sam Vogel was struck a bone

crushing blow to his skull. Perhaps the weapon was a piece of pipe; perhaps a tire iron. In any event, the weapon was never recovered. He sprawled across the entrance to his room, as the assailants wasted no time searching his clothing for money. Later, Sam Vogel vaguely remembered his assailants as the youths he had seen in the parking lot. They disappeared from the motel crime scene, never to be identified; never to be arrested; never to be brought to justice.

Within a few minutes, the seriously injured motel guest tried to gather his bearings as he regained consciousness. Eventually, he rose and managed to stumble onto the parking lot area outside his room. There, with his head bleeding profusely, he wandered about briefly in a disoriented state as the injury began to traumatize his whole body. Fortunately, another guest found Vogel and helped him. Together, they walked to the motel office, but no employee could be located. In fact, the motel office was unstaffed and locked. Finally, the good Samaritan took Sam back to his guest room, where he telephoned the authorities. Soon several police officers and an ambulance arrived. Sam was transported to a nearby hospital, where he was operated on by a neurosurgeon. The forceful blow to Sam Vogel's head had fractured his skull and resulted in a permanent partial paralysis.

Inevitably, a lawsuit resulted from the attack on Sam Vogel. Investigations revealed that the motel was located in the heart of a high crime area. Just a few weeks prior to Sam Vogel's check-in at the motel, an employee had been robbed at gunpoint. At about the same time, an adjacent fast food business was also robbed. In spite of these facts, the innkeeper made no effort to determine the level of criminal activity in the surrounding area. The court records of this case also revealed that he had failed to upgrade motel security measures for more than a decade.

The court records further showed that the motel receptionist, the only "on duty" employee at the time of the assault on Mr. Vogel, was gone when Sam and his helper appeared at the motel office. She had been delivering toilet paper to another guest. And, at the same time, the live-in motel manager had been at a nearby shopping center. Security measures were conspicuously absent. Neither the franchised owner, nor the regional franchisor, EconoLodge, had developed or put into place professional security measures to protect guests. The motel premises were accessible on foot from any direction, because there were no effective perimeter barriers. As a result, criminal trespassers enjoyed unobserved, unobstructed access. This situation is common-place throughout the industry. Yet, paradoxically, it is this industrywide absence of motel perimeter protection against trespassers that is often raised in defense of hotelkeepers sued for negligence. Hotelkeepers claim that the absence of perimeter protection is evidence that the defendant motel was in compliance with industrywide practices, therefore, such a common and usual condition is evidence against negligence. If a lawsuit goes to trial, few juries believe this assertion. As for Mr. Vogel's lawsuit, the innkeeping security expert retained by the plaintiff, characterized the vicious attack upon Sam Vogel as "a crime just waiting to happen."

Altogether, three innkeeping security experts were retained in this lawsuit; one by the plaintiff, Mr. Vogel, and two by the defendant motel.

During the course of the six-hour, three-hundred-page deposition of the innkeeping security expert retained by Mr. Vogel, each of three defense attorneys took turns arguing with, then attempting to confuse the witness. Their lack of common civility toward the witness eventually evoked a response by Al Bryant, the otherwise mild-mannered attorney for the plaintiff. The gentleman finally exclaimed in desperation: "Let me just interrupt here for just a minute. We've been going for four hours. And, what's happening here is you ask him a question, and he gives an answer. And then you come back, and you say— so in other words—and then you put in something that wasn't in your first question. You know, we're just getting argumentative. I just want to go on and finish. But, what I want to say is, let's go on and ask the man the question, and when he gives the answer, not try and rephrase it and put something else in. Let's stick with the question, and go on to the next question."

The trial began on September 9th. A federal courtroom

does not lend itself to the ploy of twisting testimony provided under oath, and as a result, plaintiff's expert provided devastating, uninterrupted testimony. In fact, defendant's attorneys chose not to offer their two security experts for testimony at trial.

On September 14, 1982, the trial jury returned a favorable verdict for Sam Vogel. The justice Sam had sought was provided by a jury award of $450,000. Through mutual pre-trial agreement by opposing parties, this case was not appealed. Judgment was entered by the court the very same day the jury rendered it's verdict.

Innkeeping Security Principles

Ostensibly, public law enforcement is reactive in practice, whereas innkeeping security is proactive. Like public law enforcement, innkeeping security embodies special knowledge attained through study and practice. It can have a significant effect in reducing the frequency of criminal attack upon the guest. This quality, however, has been largely dismissed by hotelkeepers attempting to reduce costs associated with the practice of reasonable care for their guests.

Regardless of the worthy purpose of police and security to stop crime, neither are able to do so completely. Crime, however, can be controlled and reduced to minimal levels. Indeed, it is for this purpose that the discipline of security exists.

Committing a crime results from willful misconduct. As a result, the causes of willful criminal misconduct fall within the purview of the social and behavioral sciences and theologians. Therefore, the subject area of security is concerned with the deterrence of acts resulting from criminal behavior. Crime deterrence is the objective of criminal law and the criminal justice system, as well as private security.

The deterrence of crime is either of a general nature, or a specific nature. Specific deterrence is regarded as the absence of criminal behavior resulting from arrest, prosecution, and incarceration. General deterrence is regarded as the absence of criminal behavior resulting from the *fear* by criminals of their arrest, prosecution, and incarceration. Innkeeping security is primarily concerned with the latter.

While criminal behavior can be either specifically or generally deterred, few crimes are prevented in the sense of being stopped permanently—within the definitive context of complete cessation. The deterrence of crime in one place uproots criminal activity that merely moves elsewhere. Since effective deterrence measures vary from one locality to the next, criminals are simply using common sense in moving to a more susceptible area to recommence their activities.

Some crimes, by their nature, are more difficult to deter than others. Thus, it is important for the level of deterrence to equal or exceed the level of the criminal activity to be deterred. The more equal the level of deterrence is to crime, the less risk there is to the guest. The less equal the level of deterrence is to crime, the more risk there is to the guest.

The *effectiveness* of innkeeping security measures is not well understood by public law enforcement personnel, the academic community or criminologists. The reason is that when these professionals study crime deterrence, their focus is either the individual victim of crime, or the criminal justice system. The millions of dollars in taxpayers' money spent on the study and research of crime generally ignore the effect on crime made by private security measures. As a result, this body of knowledge has generally been absent from the information reviewed by academicians, public law enforcement personnel and criminologists. This has had a serious negative impact on hotel-motel crime deterrence. This becomes apparent in reading the transcripts of sworn testimony by "experts" who are former law enforcement personnel with limited experience as security practitioners, and who are retained by defense attorneys in lawsuits related to guest security.

It is not mere speculation that violent crimes committed against hotel and motel guests can be deterred. It is a fact, capable of proof, because it has been demonstrated.

There are three principles of general deterrence of violent crime against guests: threat of detection; detection; and interdiction. They are the cornerstone of innkeeping guest security operations. These principles control violent crime by reducing the frequency of crime against the innkeeper's guest. Ultimately, one or more of these principles can be identified as the underlying factor behind all viable guest security measures. Often, they overlap one another in both practice and effect.

Honest disagreement among security experts in the innkeeping industry with regard to interpreting and applying these principles in no way detracts from their validity, any more than the disagreement about the placement of the pieces of a puzzle, affects the solution of a puzzle.

The first principle is the *threat of detection*. It embraces psychological discouragement. For instance, using closed circuit television cameras may serve as an overt deterrent, but first the cameras must be seen by the criminal before the value of this principle can be realized. The threat of detection is almost always considered in terms of the sum of security measures observed and not simply the observation of a single security measure. The greater the threat of detection, the greater the deterrent.

The second principle is that of *detection*. Examples of this principle are the use of properly trained security patrols, intrusion detection alarm systems, effective perimeter barriers, effective lighting conditions, and proper architectural and landscaping design.

The third principle is that of *interdiction*. Catching one criminal gives rise to fear by another of interdiction. The certainty of interdiction has a greater deterrent effect upon violent crime against guests than the uncertainty of punishment from the criminal justice system. In New York City, for example, it has been estimated that the likelihood of any given felon's arrest resulting in imprisonment, is roughly one in one hundred. One man, arrested for the murder of a woman at the Waldorf Astoria, was a suspect in more than 100 knifepoint robberies of guests in New York City hotels.

Few people associated with the problem of violent innkeeping crime realize that the criminal justice system is but one system of justice at play. Within the innkeeping business environment, the interdiction of criminals presents hotelkeepers and their security agents with various options. They range from removing a person from the premises, to putting such a person behind bars. It cannot be disputed that the interdiction of hotel-motel trespassers deters crime. Many potential violent crimes against innkeeping guests are deterred by the interdiction of trespassers. Yet, this fact is little known or understood by those associated with the industry's guest security practices. It is even less understood by the traveling public.

Although private property, hotels and motels are, in general, legally obligated to admit members of the public to their premises, but it is not a "public premises." The areas of the inn-keeping premises considered to be semi-public, such as the lobby or reception area, are provided by the innkeeper for the use and convenience of patrons, as well as visitors and those members of the public presenting themselves as guests. Areas of the hotel or motel premises not considered semi-public, but semi-private, are guest room corridors and hallways. Guest rooms and innkeeping offices are considered private areas of the hotel or motel.

Typically, persons entering the innkeeping premises can be defined as (1) a registered guest, (2) the visitor of a registered guest, (3) an employee, (4) an outside contractor conducting business with management, and (5) a trespasser.

The legal rights of each of these groups vary under inn-keeping laws, however, it should be kept in mind that no person can make himself a guest without the consent of the hotel or motel. Bona-fide visitors to guests may be admitted to the premises because of the innkeeper's obligation to the registered guest, not to the visitor. Additionally, it should be understood that the innkeeper may establish any lawful and reasonable rules regarding admittance of visitors, or the conduct of registered guests, while on the premises of the hotel or motel.

In almost all jurisdictions, criminal trespass is defined by statute as a misdemeanor, punishable upon conviction by an incarceration term not exceeding one year, and/or a fine of $500 or less. The key element in the successful criminal prosecution of a trespasser is his knowledge of having been on the hotel-motel premises against the will of those lawfully in charge. In most jurisdictions, this knowledge can be conveyed orally, or by properly worded signs on the hotel or motel property. The moment a person enters the innkeeping premises to commit a crime, technically that person has already committed criminal trespass. An exception would be an on-duty employee or a registered guest engaging in criminal behavior. But considering the number of violent crimes against guests, relatively few are committed by these two categories of criminals.

The vast majority of violent crimes committed against members of the traveling public within the innkeeping environment do not just happen—they are not accidents—they are planned by the criminals who commit them. It is for this reason that the security principles of deterrence are effective.

In order to commit a violent crime against the guest, the criminal must first enter, and then remain upon the innkeeping premises for some measure of time prior to the commission of a criminal act. This is true for two reasons; the criminal must assess the risks of detection and interdiction, and he must select a victim. Criminals want to commit crime with impunity, because in a hotel-motel setting their primary motivation is profit.

Since the business of criminals is crime, it is their task to determine the probability of success in their efforts. They will familiarize themselves beforehand with the targeted hotel or motel property. Members of the local criminal element who "work" local hotels or motels are often far more familiar with the premises than employees. Those who attack guests frequently have the same zip code as the hotel or motel where the crime takes place. They often use staircases to exit a hotel or motel after the commission of a crime, because this avenue of escape affords greater anonymity and diminishes the likelihood of being observed and later identified. Few guests use staircases, naturally preferring the convenience of elevators. But, very few criminals will use a staircase as an escape route without first determining exactly where it exits, and whether a staircase opens into the lobby or outside; if it is kept locked, or if it is fitted with an alarm. The design of hotels and motels permits a most fertile environment for violent criminals. These criminal entrepreneurs do not work where there is high risk. They can simply go down the highway or around the city block to stalk a motel or hotel where risk is non-existent. Criminals will gravitate to areas where the "pickins" are easy. Just as law-abiding members of society consort with those in the same occupation, so do criminals. Thus, the security reputation of a hotel or motel property becomes common knowledge among the criminal element who "work" hotels and motels and they make it a point to keep informed about their concerns of interdiction and arrest. Within the criminal network that plagues hotels and motels, there are information brokers; those who furnish information about new lock systems, the absence or presence of security personnel, and whether such personnel are armed or unarmed. Often, they will supply stolen guest room keys to their colleagues—for a price. For instance, just a few years ago, a master level guest room key to a major hotel in New York City was selling on the street for about $1,000.

In the 1970s, Ed Quinn, a dedicated and respected director of security at the Statler Hilton in Washington, D.C., was instrumental in bringing a criminal case of trespass at his hotel before the District of Columbia Court of Appeals. This Federal Appeals Court decision was of particular significance. The case was decided on December 18, 1975. Excerpts from this appeals court decision are as follows:

> Between the months of January and March 1974, appellant was seen by the Chief of Security of the Statler Hilton on approximately five occasions.
>
> On March 18, hotel security officers again noticed appellant in the hotel. At that time, she was once more observed going upstairs with a guest. She was stopped by hotel security officers and informed of the hotel policy of not allowing any unregistered guests above the lobby. She was also told of a conversation with a police vice squad officer, and was read a "barring notice."
>
> The notice said: "You are hereby notified that you are not permitted entry in the Statler Hilton. In the fu-

ture, if you return to the hotel, and gain entry, you may be subject to criminal prosecution for unauthorized entry."

On August 19, security officers were called to the fifth floor of the hotel. They waited outside one of the rooms until appellant emerged with two male companions. She was then placed under arrest.

It necessarily follows that if a hotel has the right to exclude someone, and he or she receives appropriate notice of his exclusion, that person's subsequent presence in the hotel is without lawful authority. Thus, he or she is subject to arrest for the crime of unlawful entry.

The policy is solely within the hotel's discretion and is to be invoked by it when the hotel manager or security officer concludes the person is undesirable.

The *police lack authority to bar persons from the hotel*, and evidence is absent that the police officer requested, or even suggested the hotel advise appellant she was prohibited from further entry. Appellant's other grounds for reversal, namely that the hotel policy was unreasonably and discriminatingly applied, and that the government's evidence was insufficient, are without substance. Accordingly, the judgment appealed from below is affirmed. [Italics added.]

It is of interest to note that the appellant in the decision above was represented by a relatively unknown defense attorney, Kenneth Mundy. He was to become the chief defense counsel in the 1990 drug arrest, in a guest room of the Vista Hotel, and subsequent prosecution of Marion Barry, Mayor of the District of Columbia.

Keeping criminal trespassers off the premises of the hotel or motel is the responsibility of innkeeping management. In order to accomplish this, the hotelkeeper must identify them. Before they can be identified, they must be seen. They cannot be seen if the hotelkeeper does not provide employees to look for them. Ignoring trespassers on the premises of hotels and motels is not reasonable care. Registered guests seldom loiter on the hotel-motel premises, rather, they typically are coming or going to and from the semi-public or semi-private areas. On the other hand, trespassers are on the lookout for victims and security measures. Therefore, their behavior is ordinarily distinguishable from that of the guest.

Creating A Safe Haven

It is as possible to create a safe hotel or motel environment as it is to create an unsafe one. Since prehistoric time, humankind has sought to create a secure and safe environment to protect against attack by predators—both animal and human. Indeed, as the armed, violent criminal expands his realm of influence, this need for protection becomes increasingly imperative. Yet, this age-old need for creating a secure environment has been widely dismissed by the innkeeping industry. It has ignored the relationship between the absence of security principles in the architectural and landscaping design of hotels and motels and the steady escalation of incidents of violent criminal attack upon guests. The design for a secure hotel or motel is not accidental—it is planned. The best place for it to be planned is in the blueprint stage of new construction or the renovation of existing properties. Conspicuously absent from the budgets of almost all of the major hotels and motels is money for research and development of this critical public safety issue, architectural design, which directly bears upon the personal security of the traveling public. The industry has failed to focus the attention of architects, developers and builders upon security principles in the architectural design of hotels and motels.

But this has to change. The industry's effort must be directed to the development and support of security principles in building codes for all new innkeeping construction, as well as all renovation of existing properties.

In architectural design, the principles of general deterrence of crime against the guest are expressed in providing "defensible space." Defensible space provides structural and landscaping design that are both utilitarian and aesthetic, while also providing the security necessary to discourage criminal trespassers and enhance their detection.

Examples of the application of defensible space in a hotel-motel setting include:

(1) Locating lobby rest rooms and guest room elevators within the clear and unobstructed view of front desk and bell-staff personnel—instead of isolated or remote areas.

(2) Underground garage elevators programmed so that garage elevator passengers must change elevators at the lobby level in order to access the guest room elevators.

(3) Landscaped grounds have the perimeter of the grounds protected with barriers, such as thick, thorny rose bushes. Barriers are defined as natural or structural. Structural barriers may include brick walls, or fences, wooden, or metal.

(4) Low walls and lighting effects can be used closer to the hotel or motel structure to alert intruders that they are entering areas of the innkeeping premises that are off-limits to non-guests.

(5) The lobby area should incorporate transition zones. Such zones separate the semi-public lobby area from the semi-private areas of pedestrian traffic—guest room hallways or corridors—by means of steps, lighting variations, or change in walking surface texture, such as from lobby floor tile to carpeting, or vice versa.

(6) Landscaping design that provides only low shrubbery that is close to hotel or motel structures, to avoid the conceal-ment of interlopers.

(7) Vehicular traffic is controlled through the use of speed bumps at entrances as well as throughout parking lots, to slow automobiles, and aid in the surveillance of vehicles, and their occupants.

The greater the number of unmonitored entrances, the greater the threat of criminal trespassers. By contrast then, the more monitored accessways in the structure, the higher the security level for those who use the accommodations. Whenever guest convenience is in conflict with reasonable guest security, the security of the guest must always prevail. For instance, it may be more convenient for the guest to ask for a room key at the front desk without being asked for identification. However, to issue a key without knowing that the person requesting it is, in fact, a registered guest is not exercising reasonable care. Nothing is more inconvenient for the guest than to be victimized by a violent criminal. The failure of the vast majority of hotelkeepers to act with responsibility in the protection of guests against crime has more to do with *their* convenience, than the convenience of the traveling public.

Security Officers

The innkeeping industry, like the entertainment industry, is preoccupied with appearances. It is, therefore, not surprising that when security officers are employed by hotelkeepers, they are often provided a distinctive uniform to wear. In fact, several of the major chains maintain corporate policies that mandate all security officers wear a uniform. They believe that a security officer in uniform is good public relations, although just a few years ago they believed just the opposite. The effectiveness of uniform security officers is, at best, a highly debatable issue. There have been extensive studies conducted that have concluded that uniformed police patrols have little effect on deterring crime.

The basic function of innkeeping security officers is to protect life and property. This is most effectively accomplished by detecting trespassers through surveillance and investigation. For a number of years, plainclothed security officers were known as "house detectives." After all, detection of criminals was their mission. In order to effectively deter crime, it is necessary to detect criminal trespassers. To accomplish this, security officers need to observe the movement and conduct of people—as unobtrusively as possible—without they themselves being observed. The deterrence of crime is not advanced by trespassers observing the location, number and patrol movements of uniformed security officers. Putting all security officers in uniform would no doubt be more compatible with the exercise of common sense, if all the criminal trespassers who entered upon the hotel-motel premises, also wore a distinctive uniform. In that way, the good guys and bad guys would begin their adversarial roles on far more equal terms. The anonymity of plainclothed security officers has a deleterious effect on trespassers who stalk hotels and motels for victims, because the elements of surprise and fear of the unknown, are antithetical to criminal planning and purpose.

The deterrent principle of the threat of detection can be applied by the use of properly worded and conspicuously displayed signs on the premises that state the inn is protected by patrolling plainclothed security officers.

Sadly, and somewhat comically, certain hotelkeepers, saddled with rising attrition rates among security personnel and equally rising security uniform inventories, have resorted to hiring security officers according to their size, in lieu of expertise and professional qualifications.

The work of security personnel at the property level is dangerous, even fatal. Two security officers were working for a motel in San Antonio. Initially, the officers had been armed, but management decided to save on the motel's liability insurance by disarming the officers. The men protested, citing the nature and frequency of crime on the premises, but to no avail. Thus, on the evening that the officers responded to a complaint of a prowler on the property, they did so without the benefit of the tools to protect themselves and others. During their search, they encountered a tall, lanky man. After briefly questioning him, they decided to escort him downstairs and walked to a staircase. Unknown to them, this man was no stranger to law enforcement and he was checked into the motel under a fictitious name. Once inside the staircase, the suspect pulled a handgun from his trousers. He used the officer's own handcuffs to bind their hands behind their backs, made them kneel on the cold concrete floor and ruthlessly shot both men in the head.

San Antonio police were joined by Texas Rangers in an intensive investigation of the double homicide. About six months later, a suspect was apprehended. Miguel "Silky" Richardson was arrested, tried and convicted for their murders. Twelve years after his conviction, "Silky" is still awaiting execution at the Ellis Unit in Huntsville, Texas.

The resulting lawsuit against the motel, a property operated as part of the Holiday Inn chain, was edifying. The motel defense centered on the argument that the security officers were employees, and under Texas law concerning Workers Compensation, the motel was immune from civil lawsuit. But Texas Workers Compensation laws do not protect an employer from acts considered the result of *gross negligence* and that result in death or serious injury to employees. The San Antonio attorney suing on behalf of the family of one of the decedents was able to settle the case for nearly $1 million dollars while the trial jury was deliberating.

The brutal events in San Antonio serve as a stark reminder of the inherent hazards of confronting prowlers who stalk motels and hotels. No more dangerous condition exists for a security officer than responding to a complaint about a prowler—a trespasser. At some innkeeping properties such calls come infrequently; at others, daily. The dangers of innkeeping security work are a reality of the business of innkeeping. Emergencies concerning trespassers place a premium on communication— calling for help; giving instructions; summoning police for assistance. Failure to respond, or a serious delay in responding to a complaint about suspected trespassers, can often result in great tragedy.

A Dangerous Strategy

Preceding the attack on Connie Francis, only a handful of innkeeping chains retained corporate directors of security. But following the fall of 1974, various corporate executives of innkeeping chains became keenly aware of the fact that the industry was in the throes of epidemic violent crime directed against their guests, and that the industry would soon be plagued with mounting numbers of lawsuits.

Among some chains, hotelkeepers began recruiting corporate directors of security. Unfortunately, these efforts often resulted in employing corporate security directors who were innkeeping security illiterate because they failed to promote security staff from within the industry. Instead, they hired people from the outside—from the law enforcement community. Ultimately, this situation had far-reaching consequences for the industry, as well as the public. This new breed of industry security leadership introduced a raft of spurious and faulty ideas which in time ignored longstanding reliable security principles. These new corporate security leaders soon found favor with corporate management, not by expanding reliable security principles, which would cost money—but by reducing them, and then developing a strategy to defend their negligence in lawsuits. In the long run, management figured it was less expensive to pay settlements in lawsuits than to protect the public.

This strategy was palatable to certain corporate leaders of the industry who were awakened by the Francis case. That lawsuit was viewed by these leaders as a matter of judicial interference with the operations of their business success.

The strategy reflected an attempt to absolve hotelkeepers of their historical legal responsibility for the security of the guest by the pragmatic shifting of this responsibility to the public sector—the law enforcement community.

Whenever the issue of the hotelkeeper's liability was raised in guest security-related litigation, the defense was put forth that protecting the traveling public from violent criminal attack is outside the scope and capability of normal innkeeping. Hotelkeepers would encourage the idea of complete dependence upon public law enforcement to control violent criminal attack upon the guest, while they reduced security efforts to protect guests to a mere perfunctory role.

Evidence of this strategy is reflected in the policies and practices of hotelkeepers which are antithetical to effective security efforts. This evidence includes: (1) Policies requiring security personnel to obtain approval from managers prior to arresting criminals in the act. (2) Policies requiring all security personnel to wear uniforms and name tags; (3) Policies discouraging security personnel from obtaining special police commissions in jurisdictions permitting this practice; (4) requiring security personnel to be managed by innkeeping personnel, such as the chief engineer or personnel director, who have no special knowledge of security; (5) disarming security personnel under dangerous conditions, and refusing at the same time, to train security personnel in the safe use of firearms; (on the other hand, hotelkeepers permit armored car personnel, who are armed, to walk through congested hotel or motel lobbies to pick up and deliver large sums of hotel cash); (6) using contract guard agencies to make patrol stops instead of hiring full-time security personnel; (7) maintaining security personnel manpower at the same number of staffers over many years, in the face of escalating criminal statistics, that indicate expanding security requirements; (8) scheduling security officers in the same way hoteliers schedule housekeeping or bellstaff employees—according to the house count or number of guests checked into the property. This practice is in sharp contrast to reasonable guest security, because robbery is a crime usually committed by isolating the victim. Obvious to everyone but hotelkeepers, the fewer employees and guests present on a hotel or motel property, the greater is the need for security officers on patrol. (9) Yet, another example of negligent practices is the hotelkeeper's refusal to increase security staffs while claiming that all employees are involved in the security effort, but failing to provide sufficient professional training for those employees to protect guests from crime. The careful examination of innkeeping security practices provides ample evidence that security has been relegated to a perfunctory activity—a charade—during a time of epidemic violent crime, that shows no sign of abating.

No doubt, one of the most startling aspects of this dangerous strategy is its focusing on the result, the lawsuit, instead of focusing on the cause; violent crime committed against the guest. And what permits such crime in the first place is faulty security policies and practices.

The influence of the American Hotel & Motel Association (AH&MA) cannot be ignored. Its predecessors were the American Hotel Protection Association (1910) and the American

Hotel Association (1917). In 1963, The American Hotel Association became AH&MA. It is more a federation of state associations that at the national level includes both profit-making and not-for-profit organizations. AH&MA is funded from enterprises such as the *Hotel and Motel Redbook*, a directory listing hotels and motels, *Lodging* magazine and service fees from state affiliates based on a set amount per room. Today, AH&MA represents establishments with about 1.5 million rooms.

Its influence has been forged from years of business ties that remain generally unknown. For instance, during the 1950's, AHA developed and promoted the Universal Travelcard. In 1958, this card was purchased by the American Express Company and became the basis for the American Express card. Since that time, American Express has funneled millions to AH&MA organizations, such as the American Hotel Foundation. According to an annual report of AH&MA, American Express created a "special Marketing Fund...available to AH&MA for use in developing marketing programs that benefit the lodging industry."

One of AH&MA's standing committees is one devoted to security. Traditionally, this committee has been chaired by the corporate director of security at one of the major innkeeping chains. The committee's membership is comprised chiefly of the directors of security at the elite national chains. At the same time, these security committee members seldom include a director of security with tenure and experience as a security officer at any hotel or motel. Thus, the vast majority of the membership lacks "hands on" security experience at the property level of operations. The trade association usually sends a staff member to each session of the security committee, which typically meets for two or three days about every six months.

According to the AH&MA, its charter prohibits it from establishing industry standards and will not even make recommendations about security standards. It has thwarted efforts, inside and outside the industry, to establish guest security standards because this would make its members accountable to uphold them.

Over the years, committee members have devoted a substantial amount of their time discussing guest security-related lawsuits. Typically, an entire day is set aside for this industry issue. They spend hour after hour discussing reports on the testimony their industry's defense lawyers have taken from expert witnesses. They discuss lawsuits at length. It is not unusual for copies of the transcripts of the sworn testimony of plaintiff security expert witnesses to be provided committee members for review and comment. At one meeting, an attendee suggested that corporate directors of security should communicate sensitive security information to the corporate attorney, rather than directly to executive management. Afterward, corporate counsel could report this information to the intended manager. These machinations set the wheels in motion for a future ruse, when a plaintiff's attorney requests information during discovery. At this point, the hotel or motel corporation will claim that such information is not subject to disclosure, because it is part of "privileged communication" between attorney and client.

During yet another meeting, one in attendance suggested that the circumstances of the assassination attempt upon President Ronald Reagan, just outside the VIP entrance of the Washington Hilton on March 31, 1981, might be used to defend hoteliers in lawsuits. The idea was to develop the notion that even with extra security present to protect the President, no one was able to deter the violent attack.

Of course, a number of violent attacks of particular note have occurred on or near hotel and motel properties. Theodore Roosevelt was shot in the chest leaving the Hotel Gilpatrick in Milwaukee, on October 12, 1912; Gerald Ford was attacked just outside the St. Francis Hotel in San Francisco on September 22, 1975; Senator Robert Kennedy was murdered on June 5, 1968 in the kitchen of the Ambassador Hotel in Los Angeles while seeking his party's nomination for President; and Dr. Martin Luther King, Jr. was shot and killed on the balcony of the Lorraine Motel in Memphis, on April 4, 1968. But to compare such history making crimes with crimes committed against the ordinary hotel guest is mistaken. The motivation for these crimes are too dissimilar.

Purposely, the minutes of the committee meetings are couched in general and ambiguous language, with words chosen to limit information in case the report falls into the hands of unsympathetic outsiders. Examination of the minutes of the meetings reveal the committee has sought to convey to the board of directors the need for a more effective relationship between innkeeping corporations and the *judiciary*, as well as legislators.

AH&MA offers courses to further professional development. This is achieved through the Educational Institute of AH&MA. The Institute first operated on the campus of Mississippi State, but is now located at Michigan State University. Through this institute, the industry offers correspondence courses that include security management. Security course material carries a printed disclaimer inside each publication, which states that the industry does not endorse the material content as any industry standards.

A 1993 catalog from the Educational Institute offers an employee training program that is designed to grab the attention of AH&MA members. It does not offer to help make the guest more secure, rather it admonishes hotelkeepers to "Get courtroom evidence of your commitment to hotel security." The "courtroom evidence" is presumably the certificate of completion awarded by the Institute.

The catalog does offer various learning materials, including video cassettes about security. While these tapes are professionally developed, they have evoked criticism from security practitioners within the industry because of their simplicity and failure to inform beyond a very basic level. Of course, it will take a far greater effort than correspondence courses and videotapes to assure reasonable care for the public's safety.

The industry's position, promulgated by AH&MA, and supported by industry apologists, is that each innkeeping property is different, therefore, standards of performance in guest security are not feasible or workable for such a diverse industry. Over the years, there has been no deviation from this official posture by the innkeeping industry. It has been postured so often, that even the hospitality industry's trade publications have printed the idea in articles about innkeeping security.

It is nothing short of amazing that such an explanation enjoys acceptance and has been immune from challenge. It is an absurd assertion that flies in the face of common sense.

Circumstances change—not the principles applied to them. The circumstances of violent criminal attack on the hotel or motel guest vary, change and differ from case to case. But the principles of protecting the guest remain constant and are inviolable. As an example, the principles of a secure lock that renders it safe for use on guest room doors, are outlined in chapter three, and are a standard. These principles will provide the same necessary security for the guests of a particular hotel in Philadelphia, as they will for the guests of a particular hotel in Omaha—despite whatever diverse differences that exist between the two properties. The same is true of a host of other security measures, such as the principles in the standards of secure lighting conditions.

While opposing industry security standards and accountability, AH&MA have directed their efforts in a different direction. On March 16, 1993, they issued a news release at a press conference in New York:

> Citing care and concern for the nation's many million business and leisure travelers, five national organizations have banded together to educate and inform the public about traveler safety.
>
> Led by the American Hotel & Motel Association (AH&MA), participants in the National Traveler Safely Campaign include: the American Automobile Association (AAA), the American Association of Retired Persons (AARP), the American Society of Travel Agents, (ASTA), and the National Crime Prevention Council (NCPC). The five-member coalition has a combined outreach potential to more than 100 million consumers.
>
> Kenneth F. Hine, CAE, president and CEO of AH&MA, acknowledged that the intense media scrutiny the lodging industry endured last fall (i.e., ABC's

'20/20,' CNN's 'Larry King Live') highlighted the 'critical necessity' for a public service campaign that would help travelers 'play it safe' while on the road.

Certainly, attempts to raise the level of public awareness have great merit. But the most disturbing aspect of this effort by AH&MA is that it increases the disparity between public perception and reality. AH&MA is not an association devoted to the protection of the consumer, it is a trade association committed to the advancement of its members—the innkeepers.

The goal of improving the safety and security of travelers cannot be achieved by drawing attention away from the dangerous practices of the lodging industry and instead placing the onus for improvement upon the behavior of the guests.

Unfortunately, most hotel-motel managers and owners are so diametrically opposed to the capital expenditures and labor costs associated with effective guest security measures, that the public cannot trust them to develop and administer standards of performance in guest security. Sadly, the industry's reliance on voluntary reform has produced a deepening dilemma for all concerned.

Six

The Burning Desire

Frank Hedley was an average traveler seeking a modestly priced, clean, comfortable place to stay overnight. Like other members of the traveling public, he had every right to expect the motel that he selected would be reasonably safe. However, just past midnight, April 1, 1980, Frank met his death at the hand of the most dangerous criminal who violently attacks guests—the arsonist.

A trespasser entered the enclosed, ground floor, guest room corridor of the Allentown, Pennsylvania motel and started a fire immediately outside Hedley's room. Like most arson fires, it spread rapidly, and within moments, the entire corridor was a burning inferno. It trapped dozens of guests in chaos and confusion as they tried to escape. In addition to Frank Hedley's death, twelve other motel guests were injured, some seriously.

Soon after this tragedy, the decedent's heir, as well as the surviving guests who had sustained injury, filed multi-million-dollar lawsuits against the owners of the motel. In time, by mutual agreement, the parties to the multiple lawsuits consolidated their cases, and June 1982, was set on the calendar as the trial date.

As is customary, the pre-trial discovery process involved close investigation of the policies on security at the Pennsylvania motel. Lawsuits concerning arson fires within an innkeeping environment focus on security because arson is a crime, and also carefully examine fire protection protocol because of the result of this type crime.

Pre-trial investigation dredged up some startling evidence. It was disclosed that immediately prior to this arson fire, the communities surrounding the motel had suffered a small epidemic of arson fires, with no less than six such fires having been reported. In fact, the motel had suffered a previous fire, not arson, but that nevertheless had resulted in guest injury.

Sworn testimony in this case proved that the owners and motel management had been keenly aware of the criminal threat posed by trespassers at the motel, because the motel's housekeepers had been instructed to work in pairs as a security precaution. Prior to April 1st, a number of crimes had occurred on the motel premises including two armed robberies.

The room occupied by Mr. Hedlay contained no fire emergency instructions for the guest; no sprinkler; no smoke detector. The guest room window was painted shut. A door leading from his room to the rear grounds of the motel would have ordinarily provided a second means of escape; but it had been completely panelled over. The motel's corridor, where this arson fire originated, had neither smoke detectors, nor a sprinkler system.

The motel's management, although aware of serious crimes having occurred on the premises and that an arsonist was in the area, chose not to hire a security officer to patrol the premises. Additionally, they failed to provide written fire or security instructions for their employees. In fact, only a desk receptionist and a shuttle bus driver were on duty the night Frank Hedley was murdered. To make matters worse, both were inside a motel office located across a four-lane highway that offered no view of the motel guest building which was burning about 50 yards away.

The municipal fire department station was located just blocks away, but fire fighters arriving on the scene had to lay down 1,000 feet of fire hose to reach the motel fire from the closest fire hydrant.

The motel grounds were accessible by pedestrians from any direction, since the perimeter of the motel premises lacked any natural or structural barriers to deter criminal trespassers.

Unfortunately, today these conditions still exist at many of the nation's hotels and motels. Anyone doubting this needs only to take a good look at the innkeeping properties within his own community.

In the fall of 1982, after several delays, the thirteen consolidated lawsuits against the motel in Allentown were settled, prior to trial, for $1,100,000. A source close to the case confided that the absence of adequate liability insurance was a key factor in the relatively low pre-trial settlement figure.

The death of Frank Hedley at the hands of an arsonist received only limited media attention. Few members of the industry concerned themselves with this tragedy, and members of the traveling public were not alerted by it. As a result of the pre-trial settlement, the industry's negligence was never held up to public scrutiny.

The year Frank Hedley died proved to be an especially deadly one for the traveling public. In December of that year, an arson fire in New York grabbed national headlines.

On December 4th, an arsonist entered the Stouffers Inn in Harrison, New York. The hotel provided a conference center on its premises for business meetings. The insidious arsonist poured a highly volatile liquid—with properties similar to high-octane gasoline—onto the plush carpeting of the third-floor conference area. Present inside were a number of corporate executives, participating in a high-level meeting. Almost immediately after the arsonist had ignited the flammable liquid, the area was consumed by flames, and dense, deadly smoke. This holocaust killed 26 executives and employees of well known corporations. Ironically, one of the executives was with the Nestles Corporation, the owners of Stouffers.

A few months after this tragedy—characterized as "unfortunate" by one leading industry apologist—an arsonist set fire to a guest room corridor at the Hilton Hotel in Las Vegas, killing eight people.

While the nation turned its attention to these multi-fatality arson fires, single fatality arson fires claimed the lives of guests such as Frank Hedley and received scant publicity.

Setting the stage for what was to become a public relations crisis for hotelkeepers, was a major *non-arson* fire at the MGM Grand in Las Vegas. On November 21, 1980, this fire claimed 84 lives, and injured nearly 600 people. It resulted in about 900 lawsuits, and billions of dollars in negligence claims. In short, over an eighteen-month period, 118 people died in three major hotel fires. During the aftermath and the intense debate that occurred over the fires, little attention was focused on security policies and practices—despite the fact that 34 people of the total who lost their lives had died at the hands of arsonists. The subject of security faded far into the background. It should not be inferred that it was wrong to focus on fire protection, it is necessary and desirable. But in view of the number of people who had been killed by arson, it is curious that guest security, and the deterrence of trespassers were ignored, and the 34 deaths can simply be dismissed as "unfortunate."

External Influences

The multi-fatality fires in late 1980 and early 1981 resulted in serious public debate. It bore down on industry fire protection policies and practices. This debate was joined by two distinctly different and powerful influences; professional planners of corporate and association meetings and conventions, and regulatory authorities at the municipal and state levels. During this period, many debated the issue of industry fire safety. Ultimately, these two groups provided the powerful influences that brought about positive change. Contrary to popular expectation, the industry's leadership placed a grim limit on their willingness to make the changes necessary to assure the public's safety at hotels and motels.

The economic significance of association and corporate business to hotelkeepers, especially the large chains like Best Western, Hilton, Hyatt, Marriott, Sheraton and Holiday Inn, is mammoth. Its impact is underscored by a study completed in May 1993 by the Convention Liaison Council (CLC) in Washington, D.C., a group representing 25 organizations within the meetings and travel industries. Among the key findings of the CLC study: During 1991, association spending was $53.59 billion while holding 344,000 events such as meetings and conventions; corporations spent $22.05 billion on events. This spending produced $23.6 billion in revenue for the innkeeping industry.

The industry's leadership responded to these three major fires with empty rhetoric impregnated with excuses. Industry apologists feigned collective amnesia—offering that these fires were somehow a shock; a surprising revelation. This rhetoric is inconsistent with genuine concern for the public's safety and it is inconsistent with the history of innkeeping fire disasters. Historically, the traveling public have often been victimized by hotel and motel fires. Newspaper headlines have served as stark reminders long before industry apologists were "shocked and surprised" by the major fires at the start of the '80's. On December 11, 1934, 35 people died in a fire at the Kearns Hotel in Lansing, Michigan; on September 7, 1943, 54 people died at the Gulf motel in Houston; On December 7, 1946, 119 people died at the Wincoff Hotel in Atlanta; on November 18, 1963, 25 people died at the Surfside Hotel in Atlantic City, N.J.; on March 20, 1970, 20 people died at the Ozark Hotel in Seattle; and on January 1, 1976, 20 people died in a fire at the Pathfinder Hotel in Fairmont, Nebraska.

In recent years, there has been an assumption by many that the industry's improved fire safety policies and practices are the result of renewed industry principles. But such an assumption is an error. In truth, two forces brought about the improved condition. They are: (1) Professional corporate and association meeting and conference planners who have exerted *economic coercion* and (2) municipal and state regulatory authorities who revised licensing, public assembly, and multiple dwelling laws, as well as building codes, that all resulted in revised fire code incentives. It was these two external forces that were ultimately responsible for the improved guest safety conditions enjoyed by the public and not new-found scruples by the industry's leadership.

Professional planners of meetings, conventions and trade shows for the nation's corporations and associations turned up at hotels for on-site inspections with pre-printed fire safety check lists—designed by national fire safety associations, not the innkeeping industry—and began to ask about sprinkler systems, smoke detectors and fire plans. Logically, these corporate and trade association planners booked groups of their colleagues and clients into hotels and motels that offered their guests the best fire protection; and understandably, they avoided those that did not. Even the leisure traveler appeared at the front desk of hotels and motels all across the country requesting guest room accommodations below the third floor. Joined by increasing numbers of concerned consumers, convention and meeting planners began to consider hotels and motels for reasons other than just location, comfort, or affordability.

The high-profile major hotel chains that cater to the business traveler and corporate businesses began to recognize that fire protection protocol had become, almost overnight, a competitive marketing tool and as a result of this economic coercion began to upgrade fire protection. While the average business or leisure traveler may not have understood the technology and sophistication associated with fire safety systems and protocol, he did realize the potential of being the victim of an accidental or arson fire. And he sought protection.

The high-profile major chains reluctantly embarked upon their endeavor, while the industry's leadership continued to rely completely upon voluntary industry reform and failed to develop comprehensive fire protection performance standards. This despite the fact that a staff member of the AH&MA once sat on the advisory board of a national fire association that was urging the lodging industry to develop a comprehensive program. Unfortunately, a significant portion of the industry's fire safety effort remains little more than mere window dressing and tokenism.

As an example, the very same national chain that experienced the arson fire deaths of eight people on February 10, 1981, in Las Vegas, experienced another major fire eleven months later at the Westchase Hilton in Houston that killed twelve people. The negligence of this national chain in this fire on March 6, 1982, strikes at the heart of the industry's indifference and lack of concern for the public's safety. This fire occurred on the fourth floor. When the blaze broke out, an alarm sounded at the front desk. But, because the hotel never trained the front desk receptionist what the buzzing alarm signified, he turned the alarm off—not once, but several times. Each time the alarm was turned off by the hotel employee, the alarm automatically reset to go off in three minutes. After turning the alarm off several times, the untrained hotel employee finally realized that there was a fire. This conduct played a significant role in contributing to the deaths of the guests, because of the serious delay in notifying the municipal fire department.

The fire code was not helpful because it did not mandate that hotel employees be trained. Amended in 1981, this Houston Fire Code required a fire sprinkler system in hotels; but owing to political fashion, the code was not retroactive and the hotel was exempt. So this hotel, where twelve died, had no sprinkler system in the guest room areas. Of course, the Houston fire code did not *prohibit* the Hilton chain from installing a sprinkler system in the guest room areas.

When such scandalous conditions are shown to exist in the operations of an elite national hotel chain, it is no surprise that public concern about safety in much smaller hotels and motels increases dramatically. Innkeeping fires, regardless of cause, are not confined to specific size hotels or motels; geographical boundaries or seasons.

The potential for a hotel or motel fire disaster is omnipresent. While neither the Houston Fire Code, nor any other fire codes, *prohibit* a hotelkeeper from installing smoke detectors or sprinkler systems, the ordinary hotelkeeper will not do any more than they are required or coerced into doing. This is true whether the issue of the public's safety is concerned with innkeeping fire protection, or guest security against violent criminals.

Planners face the risk of liability in booking conventions, meetings, conferences, and exhibits into unsafe hotel and motel properties. But, the professional meeting planner cannot write off his responsibility by merely booking business at a hotel or motel with reasonable fire safety features, such as sprinkler systems. The planner must go one step further; colleagues and clients must be furnished information on how to confront a fire emergency, so they know how to protect themselves. They will investigate a hotel's fire prevention program, fire detection system and fire suppression systems. And, with arson crime a serious danger to guests, during on-site inspections, the meeting planner must determine security protocol, including taking a careful look at properties in high crime locations, or those properties with a history of arson.

The next time a meeting planner conducts an on-site inspection of an innkeeping property as a prelude to booking a hotel or motel, he should ask the bellstaff or housekeeping employees when the last time their employer provided an "education program" for them. Planners should also note if the covers or caps for fire standpipe connections are missing—an overt indication of neglect by the innkeeper and a serious disregard for the safety of guests, as well as employees.

Over twenty years ago, in 1970, the U.S. Congress created the Occupational Safety and Health Act. This act created OSHA—the Occupational Safety and Health Administration of the U.S. Department of Labor. OSHA is a regulatory agency with the mission to help maintain safe work conditions for American labor. With regard to fire safety, its regulations also pertain to the giant innkeeping industry. Unfortunately, OSHA has lowered its profile to such an extent that the public has ceased to expect very much from it. Compliance with the OSHA regulations affecting innkeeping is seldom scrutinized prior to a reported incident, and the industry as a whole has often ignored adherence with the OSHA fire safety regulations which affect innkeeping operations.

Part 1910.157 of OSHA regulations pertains to portable fire extinguishers. Where employers, such as innkeepers, provide fire extinguishers for use by employees in the workplace, section "G" states in part:

(G) TRAINING AND EDUCATION.
(1) Where the employer has provided portable fire extinguishers for employee use in the workplace, the employer shall also provide an educational program to familiarize employees with the general principles of fire extinguisher use and the hazards involved with incipient stage fire fighting.
(2) The employer shall provide the education

required in paragraph (G1) of this section upon initial employment and at least annually thereafter.

While it cannot be denied that several of the large national and regional chains have improved fire safety, as well as OSHA compliance on their properties, the issue of public safety throughout the industry cannot be diagnosed or remedied by the conduct of a few national chains acting alone.

Since some fire codes came under review and revision in the aftermath of the three major industry fires mentioned, there has been a growing tendency to equate a hotelkeeper's compliance with fire codes with the exercise of the standard of reasonable care. However, such compliance is not necessarily reasonable care. Fire code regulations are minimum standards. Many fire codes are written as the result of the influence of politics. Far too many codes remain archaic. Circumstances dictate reasonable care and unreasonable care.

Consider circumstances where fire code regulations do not require a hotelier to install a sprinkler system inside a large casino—a casino roughly the size of a football field—where alcohol is served to patrons and smoking is permitted. Consider further, that a fire occurs inside the hotel, spreads rapidly into the casino, and results in many fatalities. Similar conditions did exist and such a fire did occur. The casino measured approximately 150 feet by 400 feet. Of the 84 people who died at the MGM Grand in Los Vegas, 14 were killed on the casino level, many of them inside the casino itself.

After this fire, Clark County, Nevada, adopted one of the strictest fire codes found anywhere in the U.S. As a result of this fire code incentive, the ruined hotel was rebuilt to become one of the safest hotels in the nation. Adoption of this code's standards was achieved without the industry asserting that because each innkeeping property is diverse and different, standards are neither feasible nor workable.

Interestingly enough, even municipalities are not immune from penalty. Some municipalities have been held liable for unsafe conditions which result in injury from a fire at an innkeeping establishment. For example, the New York Court of

Appeals said that a town issuing a certificate of occupancy to a motel, despite dangerous fire code violations on the motel premises, was liable for damages. In part, the Appeals Court stated: "The town had a duty, in the face of alleged blatant and dangerous code violations, to refuse to issue a certificate of occupancy."

Fire: A Lethal Weapon

The innkeeping arsonist is a most dangerous criminal, since arson at a hotel or motel often results in multiple fatalities and injuries among guests, employees, patrons, and fire fighting personnel. At one time, arson was considered such a heinous crime in England that it was punishable by death—death by burning.

In spite of recently declining innkeeping fires, the percentage of fires classified as arson has actually increased, so that arson is the leading cause of death from innkeeping fires.

There are five broad categories of arson motivation: (1) fraud, (2) psychotic behavior, (3) juvenile vandalism, (4) hiding other crimes, and (5) vengeance. They all have one thing in common: the desire to burn.

Often there is more than one motivation for the arsonist, and the categories may overlap in some arson crimes. An impressive portion of arson fires in hotels and motels are committed by employees and former employees, with vengeance playing a key role. Since "crisis hiring" is rampant throughout the industry, many applications for innkeeping positions are never properly scrutinized. Once hired, few hotelkeepers promulgate and enforce written rules and regulations regarding employee conduct to assure that off-duty or former employees are not on the innkeeping premises. From a security perspective, after the security considerations of architectural and landscaping design are satisfied, the personnel selection process is the next most important aspect of securing the premises, and protecting the guest, patrons and employees from crime.

With the exception of on-duty employees, (or registered guests, and other lawful persons on the premises, referred to in

Chapter Five) an arsonist, like other criminals who commit violent crimes against the guest, is a trespasser.

Virtually all authorities on arson agree that it is a crime rarely committed impulsively; rather it is a calculated crime, executed with considerable planning. In this sense, it does not differ from the violent crime of robbery.

Multi-fatality innkeeping fires that result in five or more deaths, classified by investigating authorities as suspicious, are found to originate most frequently in guest room corridors, hallways, and exit areas, such as guest room area staircases. Of course, these are the very same semi-private areas of innkeeping space where criminal trespassers—burglars, robbers, and rapists—can often be discovered by effective security patrols. As an example, the May 1993 issue of *Hotel/Motel Security and Safety Management* reported that two armed men evidently started a fire in the fourth floor stairwell of the Southfield, Michigan, Holiday Inn as a diversion before they robbed the front desk of the 16-story hotel.

Like other violent criminals who enter the lodging premises to victimize guests, the arsonist assesses the risk of detection and interdiction; because the last thing an arsonist desires is discovery while inflicting his nefarious crime on others. For this reason the general deterrence principles embodied in the discipline of innkeeping security are as applicable to the deterrence of arson as they are to the deterrence of other violent crimes. If this were not true, there would be no defense against the innkeeping arsonist.

Most victims of hotel or motel fires do not perish from the burns they sustain. They perish from asphyxiation. Fires emit toxic and poisonous gases. A principal product of smoldering polyvinyl chloride (plastics) is hydrogen chloride, which by itself is a toxic gas. But, when it comes in contact with moisture—in the air, on human skin, or inside the nasal passage or lungs of humans—it instantly turns into hydrochloric acid, which burns, corrodes, and kills.

Sufficient medical evidence exists, through the respiratory tract pathology reports of victims of innkeeping fires to prove that the effects of exposure to hydrogen chloride results in the erosion of the upper respiratory tract, hemorrhage, pulmonary edema, as well as etching of the cornea. In short, burning plastic is lethal. And, hotels and motels are full of plastic: upholstered furniture, floor tiles, curtains, etc.

Throughout the U.S., very few fire codes regulate the types of fabrics used in hotels or motels; and few hotelkeepers have sought to reduce the use of plastics, in order to reduce the risk of death to guests, employees, and fire fighting personnel. It is interesting to note that federal regulations restrict the materials used in the carpeting of interstate commercial aircraft, but they do not restrict the materials used in the carpeting of thousands of miles of guest room corridors and hallways.

The MGM Grand fire in Las Vegas was the subject of meticulous examination by authorities. It produced evidence that 78 of the 84 deaths were the result of breathing toxic and poisonous gases, and that approximately 60% of the hotel's furnishings contained polyvinyl chloride, or PVC. In addition to hydrogen chloride, smoldering PVC also emits other poisons, such as carbon monoxide.

The horrible hotel arson fire, in January 1986, which killed 97 people at the Dupont Plaza Hotel in Puerto Rico, prompted the U.S. Congress to pass a bill—HR 94—that prohibits reimbursement of hotel or motel costs for federal workers failing to stay in hotels that provide sprinklers and smoke detectors. Reliable sources state that the federal government spends approximately $1.5 billion annually on employee lodging. This legislation became law in 1990.

This federal legislation is long overdue. In taking this action, the federal government is simply following the lead of a number of private corporations and trade associations that have discouraged their employees from checking into unsprinklered innkeeping properties. By confusing virtue with necessity, industry leaders seemingly possess an infinite capacity to claim credit for the glacial-paced improvement of hotel-motel fire safety. Unfortunately, fewer than half of the guest rooms offered to the public by the industry today provide sprinkler protection.

In early 1991, the director of commercial travel for Sheraton Hotels, boasted that his hotel corporation had defranchised nearly 200 properties over the past three years because of non-compliance with strict corporate fire safety standards. Of course, no mention was made of dropping franchised properties because of non-compliance with corporate standards for the performance of guest security. Yet, there are more guests killed in arson fires than accidental fires.

Surviving An Innkeeping Fire

Few hotelkeepers have a written fire emergency manual, or a viable fire safety instruction program for their staff. Employee training is a matter rarely referred to in fire codes throughout the U.S.. This, despite the fact that virtually all fire safety authorities agree: it is of utmost importance that the innkeeping staff know proper and safe procedures to follow in the event of a fire in order to save lives and reduce injuries.

In considering current conditions, one becomes increasingly aware that the most intelligent course of action for the traveling public is to self-educate for protection. In doing so, business and leisure travelers can substantially reduce the risk of serious injury or death in an innkeeping fire.

For example, when a fire occurs at a hotel or motel the best place to be is outside the burning structure. Therefore, from a fire safety perspective, common sense dictates that the guest would be safest in a motel room that exits at ground level directly to the outside. The guest is next safest in guest rooms located on the second floor or below. Ordinarily, jumping from a balcony or window of a hotel or motel from the second floor will result in minor injuries; from the third floor, serious injuries; above the third floor, almost certain death.

Low-rise properties are considered to be hotels or motels of five floors or less. Low-rise properties with internal corridors and staircases for escape to the outside are considered safer than high-rise properties with internal corridors and staircases for escape to the outside. It is a foregone conclusion, however, that not all members of the traveling public will obtain the safer accommodations thus far described, either because of a lack of desire to do so or because of the absence of the availability of such accommodations upon demand. Obviously, the vast majority of the traveling public, particularly business travelers, will find themselves checked into a guest room located in the upper floors of a high-rise structure. Under such circumstances, there is certain information available to the traveler to help reduce the risk of serious injury or death in an innkeeping fire. This knowledge can be quickly divided into two considerations: (1) what the guest does immediately after checking into the guest room; and (2) what the guest can do in the event of an actual fire emergency in a high-rise.

Immediately upon arrival inside the guest room, the guest should check the windows, or balcony doors, to learn if, and how, they can be opened and closed. In doing so, the guest should look outside, to orient himself to direction or landmarks; then the guest should check the fire exit doors and staircases on the guest floor. He should make certain that they are usable and find out if the doorknob will open the exit door from the stairwell side, since fire codes vary.

Preparation is a key to survival. On the way back to the guest room, each door between the exit and the room occupied by the guest, should be counted and noted, simply because under emergency conditions it is possible that escape down the staircase may not be feasible; and therefore, returning to the room under conditions such as a lack of lighting, may require knowledge of exactly the number of doors between the occupied guest room and the exit. After observing these precautions, the smart guest checks the telephone to determine the method for calling the fire department if necessary; and then, he will place the guest room key in the same accessible place before retiring each night. An emergency is not the time to search for the room key, which should be taken in case returning to the guest room becomes necessary because escape to the outside is not possible. Since many properties do not provide smoke detectors inside the guest room, it is advisable for any traveler to carry a working battery-operated smoke detector and to place it above head level.

The guest who adheres to these precautions will be confident of safety and such confidence will help displace fear. But these considerations deal with precautions prior to notification of fire. The knowledge of safety precautions to be used during the actual notification of a fire emergency will further serve to dispel fear. This is vital, because fear is an arch enemy of survival, since it leads to panic. People get hurt and killed in a fire when they panic. To be sure, there will always be some fear. It is a human emotion that even a veteran fire fighter experiences, but it can be controlled through preparation.

Notification of fire may occur in various ways, but a most common way is through the sense of smell—the smell of smoke. Notification however, can be received as a result of the sound of fire trucks, an internal hotel or motel alarm signal or smoke detector inside the room. If a fire is in an incipient state inside the guest room, and there is any attempt to extinguish it, the fire should never be allowed to come between the guest and the guest room door. When present inside any confined area where there is fire, the safest place to breathe is close to the ground, or floor. This is because air will become hot and rise; cooler air, less contaminated, will drop toward the lowest level. If there is a fire inside the room, and the guest leaves, the door to the room must be closed tightly to confine the fire, impeding its spread. If the fire is outside the guest room, somewhere within the innkeeping structure, it is important to assess the feasibility of escaping to the outside of the building. In doing so, it is important to place one's hand upon the inside door knob of the guest room to check for heat before opening it. The door is probably wooden, and the metal door knob will indicate heat more accurately. If the door knob, or door, is even warm, the door should not be opened. There are a great many deadly gases in the hot air on the other side of the door. If it is warm, entering that air is suicide. Even if the door and knob indicate no heat, the body should be braced cautiously against the door prior to opening it; and the guest should be prepared to quickly slam it shut if necessary.

There should be no attempt to walk to the exit in a corridor that is smoky. And, of course, no one should ever use an elevator to escape. Elevators can do some very strange things under ideal conditions; but in a fire emergency, they can become vehicles of certain death, sometimes taking passengers directly to the fire floor, where either the heat or smoke will keep the elevator doors open, and the elevator immobile, trapping passengers.

If it is determined that the corridor is smoke free and escape is possible, the guest should soak a bathroom towel with water and take it along with the guest room key. The guest should be certain to close the guest room door tightly. He should walk to the exit staircase, and use the bannister for guidance, to avoid being knocked down by other guests fleeing in panic. It is possible that while descending the staircase, dense smoke will be encountered at the lower levels. This sometimes happens when the fire floor is below the point where descent is started and the door leading to the staircase on the fire floor below is kept open, and smoke enters the staircase. As the hot air and dense smoke rise in the staircase, they encounter cooler air, which stops its ascent, at least temporarily. This is called a "stack effect." Under no circumstances should anyone attempt to walk or run through a smoke stack, because survival is next to impossible.

If such circumstances occur, there are four options: (1) the guest can gain access to another guest floor above the "stacking" and use another fire exit staircase, free of smoke, to exit the building; (2) he can attempt to gain access to the building roof at the top of the staircase; (3) he can return to his guest room; (4) he can gain access to another guest floor, and try to find refuge inside another guest room. If smoke is encountered, the guest should crouch down and place the wet towel over his nose and mouth. If he decides to return to his room, or if the guest never leaves the guest room because the door knob is warm to the touch or the corridor is filled with smoke, the guest room itself can become a very safe haven in a hotel or motel fire. Under certain conditions, remaining inside the guest room is the wisest course of action.

Panic can cause confusion. The elderly and the very young are most prone to a confused state of mind during a fire emergency. They are often found by fire fighters under beds or inside closets. But such behavior is not the exclusive mindset of the senior citizen or children, as evidenced by the fact that adults who should know better, are sometimes found by fire fighters fully clothed, sitting in a full tub of water in the bathroom.

Forced by circumstances to survive inside the guest room of a burning hotel or motel, the guest who knows what and what not to do has a far greater chance to walk away unscathed from the ordeal than those who never took the time to learn.

If confined to the room, the guest should promptly use the telephone to contact the fire department and then the hotel or motel staff. Hotelkeepers have a long history of reluctance and delay in contacting the fire department. Many of them think it is poor public relations to have fire trucks pull up in the driveway. Sometimes, delayed fire fighters arrive only to observe many fire extinguishers lying around the area of the fire's origin, because employees attempted to put the fire out *before* calling for professional help. Another reason for the guest to call the fire department is that very few alarm systems used in hotels and motels automatically notify municipal fire fighters.

Once the guest has determined that escape to the outside is infeasible and that remaining inside a room is prudent, there are a number of activities to engage in that assure a period of safety while rescue is awaited. The first is to fill the bathtub with water, but not because it is going to be used to sit in. Then, the exhaust fan in the bathroom should be turned on. Next, the guest should gather bedspreads, sheets and pillowcases, as well as ice buckets and waste paper receptacles, and place all these items in the bathroom near the tub that is filling with water. These items will later serve as valuable tools of survival.

The sheets, bedspreads, and pillowcases are saturated with water by immersing them one by one in the bathtub full of water; then these wet items are torn into pieces and stuffed into the space at the bottom of the guest room door, as well as any other cracks in, or around the door. Pieces of wet material are also used to help prevent smoke from entering the guest room from any air vents. It should be kept in mind that fire fighters assigned to the rescue team will be arriving on the scene quickly and working very hard to reach all guests and take them to safety. Survival inside the guest room, by keeping out deadly smoke, is the single vital task facing the guest until that rescue is effected.

If flames are visible outside the window, the guest should remove the drapes and use the water source in the bathtub to saturate the window area with water, and keep it soaked. If no flames are visible and the window can be opened, the guest should open the window for a fresh air supply. But the guest should be prepared to close the window in the event that smoke appears outside, and wind direction shifts, blowing smoke into the room. Breaking windows presents two problems: one, in doing so, it is very possible that the falling broken glass will injure fire fighters below; and two, after the window is broken, it remains open and keeping out smoke that may later appear outside becomes a major problem. Therefore, the matter of breaking the guest room windows in case of fire warrants careful consideration. If the window must be broken, a piece of furniture can be used. If the window opens, or has been broken open, the guest should hang a white sheet outside, signaling the need for rescue by fire fighters.

While awaiting rescue, the guest must remain vigilant. The guest room door and walls should be constantly checked for heat; and if warm, the ice bucket or wastepaper basket should be used to bail water from the bathtub and onto the door and walls to reduce the temperature. If smoke is present in the room for any reason, the guest should move as close to the floor as possible, because that is where the most clear air will be found. A wet towel can be swung around the room to help clear smoke. The guest can also tie a wet towel around his nose and mouth to help him filter any smoke and breathe easier.

By implementing these measures, the guest helps reduce the risk of serious injury or death in an innkeeping fire, and increases his chances for survival.

Seven

Avoiding Untimely Checkouts

"It went in above my left breast, and exited in the back, near waist level." These were the matter-of-fact words chosen by Kathy Kadray to describe the painful path of the bullet that had ripped through her body. Her every word was recorded during a deposition in the law offices of the prestigious defense attorney, retained by a Texas hotelier. The testimony revealed the details of her abduction, in 1982, from the premises of a Houston motel. Emergency surgery left a seven inch abdominal scar that took months to heal; the psychological scars would last a lifetime.

Ms. Kadray's nightmare began at about 9:30 p.m. on a damp, foggy evening in November. After a long stressful drive from Colorado, in a rental truck packed with personal possessions, Kathy arrived in Houston, and a new job, with a sense of adventure and enthusiasm.

When Kathy spotted the conspicuous motel sign to the left of the highway, she decided to pull into the driveway and check in. She was inside the motel just long enough to register, pay cash for her room, and receive her key—a matter of five minutes or so. The motel receptionist informed the new guest that her room was located in the rear area of the comfortable, independently owned motel.

The guest walked out the large glass double doors toward her truck, which was parked perpendicular to the entrance, about ten feet or so from the motel's lobby door. As she approached her vehicle, two men suddenly appeared from behind the truck. One of them quickly placed a handgun to Kathy's head and said: "Don't scream lady, if you don't want your head blown off."

Kadray was forced to open the door to the cab of the truck and the keys were taken from her. She was struck on the side of her head, and pushed inside the truck. This all occurred within clear sight of the motel reception area.

As her assailants drove from the motel parking lot, the nightmare continued to unfold. For the next thirty or forty minutes, she was brutally sexually assaulted. Ultimately, she was driven to a remote and desolate area near a Houston ship channel and thrown out of the truck along with her suitcase, sandals, and clothes. As she attempted to gather her belongings along the roadside, her two sociopathic assailants cursed at her. Without warning, one of the assailants fired a single shot that struck Kathy in the chest, dropping her where she stood gathering her clothes. She lay semi-conscious as the truck sped off into the darkness. Fortunately, an alert security officer, patrolling the channel area, heard the shot and responded. He found the young woman, bleeding beside the roadway and summoned help. Kathy was transported to a nearby hospital, where she required surgery to save her life. No doubt, she owes her life to the conscientious security officer.

In the aftermath of this brutal crime, the Houston Police Department conducted an intensive investigation. With the co-operation of a national television network, a reenactment of this crime was filmed with professional actors. This mini-production was aired for the viewing public. Soon thereafter, the police arrested two suspects and charged them with the abduction, and various crimes associated with it. One of the defendants pleaded guilty to some charges and cooperated with the authorities.

On June 4, 1984, the other defendant, the "trigger man" in the shooting, was tried for his crime. He was subsequently convicted in criminal court, and sentenced to ninety-nine years as a guest of the Lone Star State and fined $10,000. The arrest, conviction, and sentence meted out in this case offers a more equitable finale than the outcome of many other violent crimes perpetuated against the traveling public.

Kadray retained a well-known law firm in Houston and sued the motel where the abduction had occurred. She alleged that the innkeeper failed to establish a written guest security protocol for employees; provide employees trained in security to escort the guest to her room; patrol the premises to detect and remove trespassers; and maintain alertness to oberve the assault and abduction of the guest taking place just outside the motel entrance. Although not an issue in this case, it is interesting to note that Ms. Kadray was to be roomed in the rear, isolated area of the premises. The case was set for trial in October 1986, but the motel settled the case out of court.

Kathy Kadray never saw the inside of her room. Perhaps if she had, she would have been completely safe. But, at many properties, the belief that the guest is sheltered from harm is mistaken.

In September 1991, an elderly Illinois couple was murdered at the Ocean View Resort in Portland. The assailant entered their room through an open window. In 1992, the murderer was convicted and sentenced to life in prison without parole. The couple's family is suing Ocean View Resort, Best Western International, Inc., and Miller Cook Architects for over two million dollars, alleging failure to provide proper ventilation; provide devices to safely secure the window; and keep trespassers off the premises.

As alarming as these cases may have been, in terms of sheer magnitude, few crimes equal the violent drama that unfolded in a hotel located in the historical city of New Orleans. It was an event that holds valuable lessons for today's hotelkeepers.

On a Sunday morning in early January 1973, a twenty-three year old resident of Harvey, Louisiana, drove a stolen automobile into the garage of an eighteen-story Howard Johnson's hotel in downtown New Orleans. The first seven stories of the hotel were comprised of parking spaces, with the eighth through the eighteenth floors occupied by guest rooms. At each end of the hotel structure there were fire staircases that ran from the ground level to the eighteenth floor. Not a single hotel door leading from either of the two fire staircases was equipped with security alarms. And, although each door was equipped with self-locking devices, these locks were frequently circumvented by housekeeping personnel. They placed towels between the door and its frame, to facilitate going from one guest room floor to another without use of the elevator.

Crime on the hotel property was rampant. It included burglaries of guest rooms, armed robberies of guests, assaults, bomb threats, and a possible arson fire on the twelfth floor that claimed six lives. Yet, this hotel employed no trained security officers.

After driving the stolen automobile into the garage that chilly Sunday morning, the criminal trespasser embarked upon a calculated and planned reign of violence and terror. The trespasser moved freely from room floor, to floor. Armed with a 41-caliber magnum rifle, he killed guests and set fires throughout the hotel premises. On the eighteenth floor, this gunman struggled with a doctor in the corridor. Another guest later was quoted as saying that he had heard a woman scream: "Please don't shoot my husband." The doctor was shot by his assailant in the left forearm and in the heart. His wife was shot in the head. Both died instantly. During the course of this nightmare, the gunman terrorized a surrounding five-block area of downtown New Orleans as the killer engaged in a sniping spree that left one New Orleans police superintendent and two other officers dead.

Well over one hundred law enforcement officers surrounded the hotel. Swarms of firefighters joined lawmen at the scene and attempted to extinguish numerous fires as shots continued from inside the hotel. It was difficult for anyone who witnessed it to believe that the terror was the act of a single person—but it was.

The carnage ceased at about 10:00 p.m. when the hotel gunman was flushed from a hiding place on the roof by a rain of machine gun fire from an armored U.S. Marine Corps assault helicopter. The terrorist was killed from the torrent of gunfire from the helicopter, as well as the gunfire from police sharpshooters positioned in a nearby high-rise building. The newspaper headlines of the Monday morning editions announced a grim toll: seven dead; thirteen wounded, some critically. But the final count exceeded these figures: nine died; nineteen were wounded.

And, it would be this hotel horror carried out by a madman in New Orleans that would spark the nation's big-city police departments to develop anti-terrorist and anti-hostage programs. By contrast, the innkeeping industry, as a whole, has done nothing significant with respect to discouraging such crime.

One year later, almost to the day, the first lawsuit against the hotel was filed in the U.S. District Court, asking $6,205,000 in damages for the heirs of a couple killed by the arson-sniper. Other lawsuits were filed by guests from Jonesboro, Georgia, and Hot Springs, Arkansas. The hotel and its insurance carriers paid out enormous amounts in claims and the hotel had to be renovated before re-opening for business. Today, no hotelkeeper cares to remember this crime; reference to it is conspicuously absent from industry material regarding security matters.

According to an informed source, after this terrible tragedy, a very significant piece of evidence surfaced. A search of the residence of the man killed on the hotel rooftop produced handdrawn sketches and diagrams of the interior layout of the hotel; evidence that the killer had visited the hotel premises at least once prior to acting out his brutal crime. Like most criminals, he planned his crime carefully—assessing security beforehand. No doubt, he was encouraged by its absence.

Astute observers of industry security still refer to this tragedy as a good example of the vulnerability of the nation's hotels and motels to terrorism in today's international political climate.

Standards

The aim of safety for the traveling public cannot be achieved by a few innkeeping chains, acting in isolation. The disturbing absence of clear industry standards for the performance of guest security, around which hotelkeepers can mobilize resources has directly contributed to the problem. It is obvious that the industry cannot be completely relied upon to develop standards and implement them; therefore, it may be necessary for federal legislation to be enacted. Such legislation should address:

(1) The development and implementation of industry standards for the performance of guest security.

(2) The requirement that hotelkeepers maintain accurate records of all crimes committed upon the hotel or motel premises. This must be done regardless of whether or not those crimes are reported to law enforcement authorities.

(3) The public disclosure of these records, upon demand, to anyone seeking accommodations.

(4) The Uniform Crime Reporting program of the U.S. Justice Department should be expanded to include the indexing of crimes related to hotels and motels.

For those innkeeping establishments that are engaged exclusively in intrastate commerce, state legislation should be enacted that embodies these improvements.

It is to be expected that the industry would act to mobilize opposition to such legislation. After all, the industry's apologists have never relented in their clumsy effort to minimize the responsibility of hotelkeepers to provide safe lodging for the public. The best argument in favor of legislative action is the evidence demonstrating beyond any reasonable doubt that voluntary reform has failed to provide reasonable care to protect those who use the accommodations hotelkeepers offer.

No influence upon the industry's security can have a more expedient and positive effect than economic sanctions. The traveling public, as well as professionals within the hospitality industry, such as professional planners of corporate meetings, should simply cease rewarding negligent innkeepers. Hotelkeepers who demonstrate public responsibility by refusing to place profits before principles, should be sought out, rewarded and patronized.

There clearly can be no justification for corporate and association meeting and convention planners to book business into the hotels and motels of innkeepers whose managers demonstrate indifference to the public's safety. As professionals, planners have both a moral and legal responsibility to be certain that their clients or colleagues are safe and secure in hotels and motels. This responsibility is rudimentary, and understood by some corporate and association planners who have already embarked upon a policy of avoiding unsafe innkeeping properties. This is to their credit. It has been largely the result of the recent shift from staff planning within corporations and trade associations, to outside consultants.

Other members of the hospitality industry, such as professional travel agents, pose yet another concern. Many travel agents serve as a precarious catalyst by booking travelers into unsafe hotels and motels. Their role, like planners, must be to assure that they reduce the risk of harm to their clients. It should be realized that a number of the nation's travel agencies are owned, directly or indirectly, by corporations that operate hotels.

The American Automobile Association (AAA) rates thousands of hotels and motels in its tour books. In 1993, AAA announced that innkeeping properties that do not comply with its new security requirements, such as dead-bolt locks on guest room doors, will be dropped from their 1995 tour books. Inspections of properties by AAA were set to begin in August 1993. It is interesting that hotelkeepers have been content to see other business organizations apply security standards to the innkeeping industry.

For many years, hotelkeepers as a whole, have endeavored to create a public image of their properties as a kind of oasis—a secure sanctuary along the traveler's journey. Some innkeeping properties may qualify as such; most do not.

Some Security Tips

Because of the innkeeping industry's advertising that implies protectorship, and the guest's preoccupation with the purpose for his travel—business or leisure—the last idea in his mind is that he will be selected as a victim of a violent crime while staying at hotels or motels. But due to the extent and seriousness of the industry's security problems, it has become increasingly incumbent upon the traveling public to intelligently modify behavior in order to help reduce the risk of becoming a victim of violent crime.

The tortoise has been provided a strong, sturdy shell; the skunk, a startling odor; the porcupine, sharp bristles; the chameleon, alterable colors. Throughout the Animal Kingdom, nature has provided its members with a means of protection and defense. The protection and defense provided to humans is intellect. It is in the expression of superior human intelligence, that civilized citizens protect themselves from the uncivilized criminal predators within society.

Intelligent modification of behavior is based on reducing vulnerability. Reducing vulnerability requires common sense awareness, an intelligent plan and faithful implementation of the plan.

Reducing vulnerability starts in advance of the traveler's journey. Advance reservations should be made for hotel or motel accommodations whenever feasible, to afford the traveler the safest and securest lodging available. Unfortunately, the same lack of knowledge that precipitates the need for answers, often limits the ability of the traveling public to ask the appropriate questions of hotelkeepers. For instance, inquiry should be made with respect to such critical concerns as dead-bolt door locks, "peep holes" in guest room doors, security staffing, and whether the property is located in a high crime area. All these concerns bear upon the traveler's vulnerability in strange surroundings. If the traveler decides to wait until arrival at his destination, few options may be available. If lodging accommodations are arranged through the services of a travel agent, the traveler should require that such questions be asked by the agent before choosing accommodations. In light of escalating violent crime in society, and the fact that it is the guest's safety and security at issue, the traveler should make such inquiry unhesitatingly. The guest is the customer, paying the bill. And in many instances, it is a hefty bill.

Further preparation for the journey includes taking only

a minimum of cash, and only enough traveler's checks and credit cards necessary to cover the journey's anticipated expenses. Rather than trust a short memory, it is wise to trust a long pencil, to write down the name and identification number of each credit card for use on the trip. Jewelry and other valuable property should be photographed for identification prior to departure, so that if robbed, positive identification can be established. It is also smart for the traveler to carry what is called "bait money"—that is, a selected denomination of paper currency from which the serial number has been recorded. This "bait money" is kept with other cash, but is not used during the journey. It facilitates the identification of any money taken from the traveler. This practice can be most helpful to authorities in their investigation of a robbery, when a suspect is apprehended in the immediate aftermath of the commission of the crime. Whenever possible, keep credit cards, travelers checks and cash in separate places—not all in one pocket or wallet. Under no circumstances should the traveler brandish large sums of cash or numerous credit cards in public. Some travelers make a fetish of displaying premium credit cards to cashiers. Such a display, for whatever reasons, is foolish and dangerous.

The traveler should check-in and check-out of an innkeeping establishment during daylight hours. Of course, this cannot always be done, especially on business trips, but it is safer.

If the selection of lodging prior to departure was not possible or desirable for some reason, remain vigilant in selecting accommodations when arriving at the destination. Most travelers will ask law enforcement personnel for directions without hesitation, but they seldom think to ask about crime in their new surroundings. Such inquiry should be made. It costs nothing, and law enforcement personnel are helpful to the traveling public. Officers have traditionally shown a willingness to direct travelers to safer sections of their jurisdiction.

The traveler is ordinarily limited in determining the safety and security of the innkeeping premises. A "walk in," someone seeking accommodations without advance reservations, has their choices somewhat circumscribed, and this is another reason why it is wise, when possible, to make advance reservations prior to embarking upon a journey. Without advance reservations, it is important for the traveler to ask the front desk personnel about safety, because of the need to determine vulnerability. This need is not diminished because of the absence of a room reservation. Innkeeping is a highly competitive business, with hotels and motels often found to be clustered in close proximity to one another. Stopping and making inquiries at various properties in a given area, and selecting the safest and securest, could well be a life and death decision.

Motels that are poorly lighted and located in isolated areas, should be patronized with caution, if at all, because robbery by force is a crime in which the perpetrator seeks out an isolated victim. The same is true of rape and often the two crimes are connected. It should also be kept in mind that the violent crimes of murder and felony assault are frequently associated with the crime of robbery.

In motels, guest rooms are usually safer when selected close to the front office reception area. Avoid guest rooms in rear, isolated areas of motels. Women traveling alone should insist upon being accompanied to the guest room upon check-in; and any refusal by innkeeping personnel to respond favorably to such a request should prompt the guest to leave the premises and seek accommodations elsewhere.

Guest rooms should be sought that are as close to the guest room elevators as possible. The less time the guest spends walking the hallways to and from his room, the less is his vulnerability to attack by trespassers.

Before boarding the elevators, observe all passengers and if uncertain about any occupant, the elevator should not be boarded. It is wise to board last and select floor buttons last. If possible, position yourself near the elevator control panel; and if attacked inside the elevator, push as many of the floor control buttons as possible.

While on board awaiting the passenger elevator to function, if joined by a suspicious appearing person, immediately exit the elevator. Before leaving the room, look carefully for suspicious persons or conditions in the corridor. In motels, scrutinize the parking areas outside before leaving the room.

After checking into a hotel or motel and upon arrival at the guest room, be sure to check six basic guest room security conditions: (1) the guest room door lock is examined to make certain it is functioning properly with a dead-bolt feature, and that the lock engages when the door is closed; (2) the bathroom and closet are checked to make certain no one is hiding—a look behind shower curtains is appropriate. (3) all windows and door locks are checked for proper function—in some instances they may be located behind drawn drapes, and the guest may not even be aware of a patio door without inspection; (4) the lock on any adjoining doors to connecting guest rooms is checked to be sure there is a lock, and that it is functioning to keep someone in an adjoining guest room from entering; (5) the telephone in the room is checked to make certain it is in working order; (6) look for any information inside the room pertaining to fire safety or security, and read the information carefully. If unclear, ask for clarification from management.

If any of the locks on windows or doors are not working properly, request another guest room immediately. If one is not available, check out.

Do not check into innkeeping properties that fail to provide a telephone inside the guest room.

For a nominal price, a portable, commercial lock designed for use inside the guest room can be purchased by travelers. It keeps the door closed, even when someone with a key tries to enter. Hotels and motels without room locks with the dead-bolt feature should be avoided. It is conceivable, however, that a traveler may not be able to avoid staying at a hotel or motel that does not provide a lock with a dead-bolt and a portable locking device can help the guest reduce vulnerability to violent crime and an unexpected check-out at the hands of a violent criminal.

While inside the room, close the door tightly and *always* lock the dead-bolt, regardless of the length of time inside. The guest room door must never be opened for anyone, unless the guest is *absolutely* certain it is completely safe to do so. The typical guest is prone to automatically open the door when someone knocks because he thinks he is safe and secure inside hotels and motels. This is a very dangerous habit. Criminal trespassers are known to don innkeeping uniforms and pose as plainclothes security or maintenance personnel to gain admittance to occupied guest rooms. Call the front desk to verify the identity of all employees.

Use the viewing port, commonly referred to as a "peep hole," before admitting anyone. The absence of a "peep hole" is an indication of negligent innkeeping conditions.

Under no circumstances should the door be opened under the assumption that the room door security chain will prevent an intruder's entrance. By design, definition and purpose, the security chain is not a lock. The security chain or bar installed on guest room doors is unreliable in keeping an intruder out if he is prone to gain entry by force.

When temporarily leaving the guest room, the television can be left on, with the volume moderately audible to someone just outside the door. A light left on at night is cheap security. Depending upon the quality of the lock on the door, it may be unwise to use a plastic "Do-Not-Disturb" sign on the outside doorknob. Such signs can be used to easily open an unsafe lock. But the overall effort by the guest, especially in motels, is to make the guest room appear occupied during a temporary absence. No guest wants to return to his room and find an intruder who used a room key to enter because no one was inside to dead-bolt the door lock. When absent from a motel room at night, the drapes should be drawn, with a light on. Plastic "Maid Requested" signs should not be used on the outside of the room regardless of whether or not the guest remains in the room.

Whenever the guest must carry large sums of cash or valuables, use the innkeeper's safe. The guest, however, should require privacy when availing himself of this service and request an escort by security personnel or management while transporting valuables from the guest room to the innkeeper's safety deposit vault. For valuables that cannot be accommodated in such a vault, such as large, valuable musical instruments or computer equipment, require management to dead-bolt the guest room door during periods of absence.

There is safety in numbers. Travelers generally reduce vulnerability when accompanied by others. If the guest is alone on the hotel premises and has reason to expect trouble, he should walk quickly to a place where there are other people, such as the lobby area.

Parking areas pose many potential dangers. Select parking in well-lighted and busy areas. When forced to park in dark or isolated areas, such as underground facilities, request to be accompanied by a security officer or staff member of the inn. Park as close to the exit as possible, to avoid walking distances across parking areas. When approaching the car, alertness is vital and car keys should be in hand, ready to use.

Women should carry their purses close to their body—not hanging loosely by the straps—with a firm grip kept on the purse. They are well advised to carry their wallet separate from their purse; inside coat pockets if possible.

Ostensibly, it is unwise to resist a criminal who is only after property or one who has a weapon. But, with increasing frequency, criminals physically attack their victims without provocation. To resist when physical assault is imminent is not a decision that can be recommended with metaphysical certitude. But if the victim decides to stop an attempt by a criminal to do bodily injury, resistance and escape should have the purpose of distraction or incapacitation.

It is important that, when caught by surprise, the victim should keep his wits about him, and use each moment to form a mental picture of the attacker's physical description: size, sex, race, clothing, etc., including his footwear. Footwear can make a lasting impression upon a victim and criminals rarely discard footwear they have worn at the scene of the crime. Where automobiles are used in a crime, identification of license numbers, makes or colors are most helpful to investigative authorities.

Animal lovers will find hotels and motels that accommodate a canine desirable to patronize. A large note taped on the guest room door announcing the presence of a canine inside the guest room can reduce the vulnerability of a guest; serving as a formidable deterrence. Besides, the four-legged family member will no doubt enjoy being with a safe guest because a safe guest is a happy guest.

Beyond Statistics

No assessment of the industry's guest security practices can be endured without exploring its peripheral effect on the employee.

Daniel Hope was a talented twenty-two year old, who studied concert piano under the direction and guidance of a world renowned music professor. He was a handsome young man, with a slender six-foot frame. Duke, as he was known, had worked his way up to being head cashier at the 270-room hotel in Bethesda, Maryland, a suburb of Washington, D.C., that was franchised as a Holiday Inn.

On Thursday, February 19, 1976, at approximately 10:00 a.m, Duke was returning to the hotel underground parking garage in his gold colored Opel after a trip to a nearby bank to make a deposit and obtain $200 in coins for use by the hotel cashiers. The following excerpts from police investigative reports attest to what befell Duke Hope:

> After exiting his auto, Hope was apparently accosted by an unknown person with robbery as the motive. There appears to have been a struggle during which Hope was shot. Projectile passed through Hope's body, ricocheted off a concrete pillar and came to rest under a large trash container.
> On 2-19-76 the deceased was discovered in the stairwell of the inn by a fellow employee.
> Hope's body may have been dragged into the stairwell as indicated by scuff marks on his shoes.
> The deceased [sic] broken eyeglasses and keys were also located within close proximity of each other.

Seventeen years earlier, Duke's mother, Doris Michaud, experienced the loss of her seven year old daughter at the hand of a drunk driver. She was devastated by the sudden shock of her son's murder. No doubt, the worst news a parent can hear is about the death of one of their children. As the details of Duke's murder unfolded, it was quickly realized that Mrs. Michaud had also become the killer's victim.

Soon after Duke's murder, the innkeeper informed Mrs. Michaud that her son had been given a small loan from the hotel, which was to be paid back in weekly installments. Since Duke was gone, the innkeeper wanted his mother to pay the balance of this loan. Mrs. Michaud promptly did so. In addition, through his attorneys, the innkeeper opposed payment to Mrs. Michaud under Workers Compensation. He argued at a hearing that she was not the decedent's dependent. But the State of Maryland determined she was at least a partial dependent. The attorney Mrs. Michaud had retained advised her that she could not sue the hotel for negligence in her son's death. In heeding this advice, she was deprived of ever knowing what a trial jury might have thought about the fact that the innkeeper later hired an armored truck courier to perform the work for which Duke was killed. Or the innkeeper's failure to provide trained security personnel on the premises the day her son was murdered, although serious crime was not unknown at this hotel.

On the day Duke was murdered, the police investigation included broadcasting a lookout to banks in the area for anyone seeking to exchange a quantity of wrapped coins for paper currency. Detectives were notified of a male subject who sought to do just that in a savings and loan located in Southwest Washington, D.C. The police were able to identify the subject through a police spread of photographs shown to the employees of the savings and loan. This identification provided police with a suspect who had an arrest record that included armed robbery. In addition, police investigative reports concerning previously stolen automobiles from the hotel garage revealed that two of them had been abandoned and recovered by the police in the vicinity of the residence of their suspect. The following are excerpts from the investigative reports of the police concerning the suspect's arrest:

> On 2-19-76 it was determined that Hope left the bank after being given $200.00 in quarters, and dimes which were wrapped in rolls and carried in a white canvas bag.
> Hope traveled back to the inn and parked his ve-

hicle, a gold Opel, in the underground parking garage near the location where his body was found.

A crime scene search was conducted and disclosed that the aforementioned rolled coins and bank bag were missing.

As a result of the missing coins, information was broadcast by local radio stations alerting businesses to be aware of anyone cashing a large amount of coins.

On 2-20-76 information was received by the police concerning a transaction which took place at [the savings and loan] in Southwest, Washington, D.C. The information concerned a male exchanging a large amount of rolled coins for currency at approximately 1300 hours on 2-19-76. Interviews were conducted with three tellers of the savings and loan. A teller related a male entered the [savings and loan] on 2-19-76 approximately 1300 hours and placed several wrapped rolls of quarters and dimes on the counter, which he carried in a dark blue or black knit watch cap. He also removed two or three rolls of quarters from his coat pocket which he placed on the counter. The teller noticed that the wrappers were loose and appeared to have been dropped. She exchanged the coins for U.S. currency, and gave the male $175.00. The male indicated he thought he had given her more than $175.00, and began searching his pockets. The teller noticed that his right pocket was weighted down with something heavy which he did not remove. Due to the subject acting suspicious, the teller was prompted to turn on the security camera, but the male exited hurriedly, without counting his money. The coins and wrappers were taken to the Identification Section and the wrappers were processed for latent finger prints. Latent finger prints were developed on the wrappers. Some of the latents were positively identified as belonging to the teller at the bank that gave the $200.00 in quarters and dimes to the deceased.

Numerous photographs were shown to the teller of possible suspects who resembled a composite drawing.

On 2-25-76 the teller viewed approximately 220 photographs and positively identified a photograph of [a suspect] who came into the savings and loan on 2-19-76 and exchanged the rolled quarters and dimes for U.S. currency.

As a result of the positive identification made by the teller, a photographic array consisting of eight similar males was shown to tellers on 2-25-76, separately, and the photograph of the subject one teller stated as looking like the male subject, and the other teller stated the photograph to be the same male. It has been determined, through Metropolitan Police Criminal Records [the subject] is 25 years, 5'10" and resides in Washington, D.C. He has a prior arrest record for assault with intent to rob, carrying a deadly weapon—gun, robbery and parole violations. On 2-26-76 the investigators applied for and were issued an arrest warrant charging [the subject] with the murder of Daniel Hope.

The police did a professional job, and delivered a solid suspect to the prosecuting attorney's office. The suspect waived extradition and was held in jail in lieu of posting bond. The county grand jury subsequently handed down a thirteen-count indictment of the suspect that included counts of robbery and murder of head cashier Daniel Hope. The trial date was set for June 26, 1976 in the county criminal court.

During his incarceration, the taxpayers provided the defendant with two defense attorneys. The defendant professed his innocence. He said that he had never been inside the savings and loan in Southwest, Washington, D.C. and had nothing to do with the robbery and murder of Duke. The defendant produced two witnesses that claimed he was at his residence with them on that unseasonably warm February morning when Duke had been shot and killed. These witnesses were his mother and girlfriend. The defendant was given a polygraph examination which he passed. Without explanation, the prosecuting attorney dropped all the charges in the thirteen-count indictment. To this day, the murder of Daniel Hope remains unsolved.

There is no conveniently concise explanation for the grief Mrs. Michaud has endured all these years. The dog-eared pages of a local newspaper describes the sordid story and includes pictures of a distraught mother picketing the prosecuting attorney's office. But the prosecutor never justified the reasons for his official conduct in this case. It remains a mystery.

The statute of limitations precludes the possibility of a civil lawsuit. The innkeeper is still conducting a successful hotel business. The attorney retained by Mrs. Michaud is today enjoying a comfortable law practice. The whereabouts of the original suspect is unknown. The earthly remains of Duke Hope are buried in a Maryland cemetery. As for Doris Michaud, the series of injustices endured by this courageous woman remain etched in her mind.

For the past seventeen years, on the anniversary date of her son's death, Mrs. Michaud has made a pilgrimage to the hotel. With uncommon fidelity, this devoted mother places a long-stem rose upon the staircase in the garage where her son died. Then, in the silence, Mrs. Michaud prays. It is difficult to overcome loneliness and pain. It is impossible to destroy love.

Afterword

The security of guests hasn't improved much in recent years and there is no promise that the situation described in this book will change soon.

Although industry advertising implies safe conditions, it is wise to be cautious and assume that hotels and motels experience crime on their premises. Therefore, travelers are advised to, at a minimum, check for:

- Limited access into the hotel-motel structure, as well as the grounds surrounding it. Generally, the more limited the access, the less likely trespassers will enter.
- Well-lighted interiors, parking facilities and grounds.
- Valet parking is preferable to self-parking. The interior parking garages should not have elevators that carry passengers directly to guest floors. A trained employee should be on duty to help protect guests and well-marked emergency telephones should be installed throughout parking areas.
- Fire sprinkler systems in lobbies, hallways, corridors and meeting rooms.
- Smoke detectors inside the guest room, as well as hallways, corridors and meeting rooms.
- Dead-bolts that are a feature of the guest room door lock.
- Viewing ports (peep holes) in guest room doors.
- Telephones permitting outside direct dialing.
- Secure locks on windows, connecting doors to adjoining rooms and patio doors.
- Staffing of personnel trained in guest security available to escort guests to their room or automobile upon request.

About the Author

Kenneth Lane Prestia has devoted most of his adult life to the security profession. His experience within the innkeeping industry includes tenure with Hilton Hotels, Howard Johnson's Motor Lodge, Western International Hotels and Hyatt Hotels.

Mr. Prestia is a 1968 graduate of the Law Enforcement School of the U.S. Department of Justice, Bureau of Narcotics and Dangerous Drugs. In 1974, he became a founding member of the Hotel Security Association of Washington, D.C., and one year later, he was elected president. Mr. Prestia is a former member of the Security and Safety Committee of the American Hotel & Motel Association (AH&MA) and he has completed the prescribed course of study of hotel-motel law. He was certified as an instructor in security management by the Educational Institute of AH&MA. Mr. Prestia was designated a Certified Protection Professional by the Professional Certification Board of the American Society for Industrial Security (ASIS) and he was appointed Chairman of the Standing Committee on Restaurants and Lodging for two consecutive years. He has been a guest speaker before corporate and trade associations, including state affiliates of AH&MA, ASIS and Meeting Planners International. Mr. Prestia has also been a guest lecturer at Cornell University.

He is recognized as an expert witness in federal and state courts concerning the security of property and the protection of persons against criminal assault. Mr. Prestia has testified for clients of either defense or plaintiff attorneys in various jurisdictions. He is also a recognized authority on inventory loss prevention, the protection of assets and the deterrence of criminal behavior.

The professional honors of Mr. Prestia include awards and commendations from the Chief of Police and the Fire Chief of Washington, D.C., as well as the Federal Bureau of Investigation and the U.S. Secret Service, for his assistance to these public agencies during his security management career. The professional affiliations of Mr. Prestia have included membership in the American Society for Industrial Security, the National Fire Protection Association, the American Hotel & Motel Association and the International Association of Chiefs of Police.